155

Harper/Hazelden Titles of Related Interest

The Twelve Steps of Alcoholics Anonymous: Interpreted by the Hazelden Foundation, Hazelden
The Little Red Book, Hazelden
Of Course You're Angry, Gayle Rosellini and Mark Worden
Strong Choices, Weak Choices: The Challenge of Change in Recovery, Gayle Rosellini and Mark Worden
Getting Sober!, Priscilla Cane
A.A.: The Story, Ernest Kurtz
Holding Back: Why We Hide the Truth about Ourselves, Marie Lindquist
The Serenity Principle: Finding Inner Peace in Recovery, Joseph Bailey

Relax, Recover

STRESS MANAGEMENT FOR RECOVERING PEOPLE

Patricia Wuertzer and Lucinda May

PERENNIAL LIBRARY

A Harper/Hazelden Book

Harper & Row, Publishers, San Francisco

Cambridge, Hagerstown, New York, Philadelphia, Washington
London, Mexico City, São Paulo, Singapore, Sydney

FIRST HARPER & ROW EDITION PUBLISHED IN 1988.

Library of Congress Cataloging-in-Publication Data

Wuertzer, Patricia.
  Relax, recover.

  (A Harper/Hazelden book)
  Bibliography: p.
  1. Substance abuse—Relapse—Prevention.   2. Stress
(Psychology)   I. May, Lucinda.   II. Title.
RC564.W83 1988   616.86'06'019   87-46219
ISBN 0-6-255482-4

---

88 89 90 91 92 HAZ 10 9 8 7 6 5 4 3 2 1

To our husbands
Stan Wuertzer and Tom Segar

CONTENTS

Chapter One   Stress 1

Chapter Two   Hostility 13

Chapter Three   Grief 27

Chapter Four   Relapse 39

Chapter Five   Needs and Choices 49

Chapter Six   Support 61

Chapter Seven   Exercise 79

Chapter Eight   Meditation 91

Chapter Nine   Relaxation and Biofeedback 97

Chapter Ten   Purpose and Meaning 111

The Twelve Steps of Alcoholics Anonymous 123

Notes 125

Bibliography 129

Index 135

ACKNOWLEDGMENTS

There are many people who contributed to this project. We owe them all our thanks. In particular we would thank Dr. Kathleen Dracup who served as our medical authority. Her friendship and support, as well as professional expertise, were much appreciated. We also thank Louis Pellitier for his advice: "A good story line and lots of sex!" Cathey Pinckney provided technical support, and Patricia Edlefsen and many others contributed support and helpful suggestions. Tom Segar performed above and beyond the call of duty in helping us prepare this manuscript. The staff at Hazelden Educational Materials was patient and encouraging to us.

CHAPTER 1

Stress

Stress exists both within and outside of us. It is present in some form whether we are awake or asleep. We experience stress even before birth and are not free of it until death. Stress affects us in many ways — socially, psychologically, physically, emotionally, and spiritually. We experience it on both conscious and unconscious levels. Since both positive and negative experiences cause stress, memories can trigger stress responses in us, as well as expectations of events to come. Stress can be as concrete as an injury, as abstract as free-floating anxiety, as momentary as a line at the check-out counter, as prolonged as grief over the death of a loved one, as superficial as not finding a parking place, and as profound as a fatal illness. Stress can be as personal as a spiritual awakening, as global as war, and as inevitable as aging. Stress even occurs at joyous occasions such as the birth of a child, a holiday get-together, or a long-awaited promotion.

We each experience stress differently because we each have unique characteristics — physically, emotionally, psychologically, and spiritually — that influence our perceptions. As our understanding of stress grows, we recognize its pervasive nature. Being "stressed out" is a common complaint heard in workplaces across the country. As more and more research indicates that stress figures both directly and indirectly in the development of disease, stress is of concern to every one of us. It is a paradox of modern life that we can't seem to live without stress, nor can we live with it. Although we can't escape stress it is comforting to realize that one reason we can't live without it is that it is often a warning signal to take some positive action.

Stress is a component of disease. The word "disease" is just that, dis - ease, a *dis*ruption of health, lack of ease. It is something we all face, from a mild case of the flu, to life-threatening diseases such as cancer and chemical addiction. There are acute diseases, like chicken pox, which appear suddenly and usually go away within a short time. There are chronic diseases, like alcoholism, that take much longer to develop and do not go away. There are primary diseases, like AIDS, which cause secondary diseases, like pneumonia. Many people believe all levels and types of disease are affected by stress.

Most of us will face a medical crisis in our lives or in the lives of those we love. These crises are frequently directly related to the amount of stress we're under; they create an enormous amount of stress in their wake; and the aftershocks can continue to stress us long after the events have occurred.

The term "stress management" implies two things: (1) stress is inevitable, and (2) we can use stress to change our lives for the better. How? By changing our perceptions of stress and its relationship to our lives. This involves education, self-awareness, and planning.

Stress management is of special importance to people in recovery from alcoholism and other drug addiction. It is a fundamental part of relapse prevention. Let's look at those two words, *recovery* and *relapse*. When we recover something, we take it back; we gain lost ground. Addicts recover their health. When we relapse, we lose ground that we worked so hard to regain. We become self-destructive again. We haven't learned from our past to manage the pain in our present or to plan for the future. Stress plays a very important role in the process of recovery; thus, if we learn to manage our stress, we can use it to prevent relapse and enhance recovery.

This book is written to give you the information you need to learn from your past and plan for the future. We ask you to take a look at your past behavior and isolate the issues and events that have caused the most stress for you. Then, through self-help tools included in each chapter, we ask you to plan changes that will interrupt your stress cycles. We encourage you to act on those plans in a responsible way with the appropriate support. The principles of stress management described in this book reflect the Twelve Step programs of Alcoholics Anonymous and allied groups. Stress management is not easy, fast, or fun. Change takes time. Stick with it. You're not alone.

Understanding Stress

Early in this century, French scientist Claude Bernard developed the concept of "milieu interieur" which means the internal environment of the body. In order for the systems of the body to do their jobs — the heart to pump blood, the digestive tract to break down food, and the lungs to take oxygen — there needs to be little or no interference. Undisturbed, our bodies take care of us as they are designed to do. The American physiologist Walter Cannon used the term *homeostasis* to define this harmonious internal environment. Our bodies work hard to maintain homeostasis.

Dr. Hans Selye brought the concept of stress to public attention.[1] When demands are made on us, the body wants to take care of the situation and return to normal. This process is the basis of Selye's definition of stress. According to Selye, "Stress is the nonspecific response of the body to any demand made upon it."[2] Any demand, positive or negative, large or small, that interferes with homeostasis is stress because the demand requires the body to adapt in order to regain its normal harmony.

Our bodies are endowed with an alarm response that helps us adapt as quickly as possible. This complex reaction is called the *fight or flight response,* and was identified in the 1930s by Walter Cannon who laid the foundation for Selye's work. When presented with a demand, the body quickly prepares for change. When you need the strength and speed to fight or flee from a threat, you've got it. This response is fundamental to survival throughout the animal kingdom, and is found at every level, from single-celled amoeba to human beings.

Individuals possess this response, and, as indicated by Selye, so do whole societies. The following is a list of changes that your body goes through when a threat or demand is perceived.

- Your heartbeat increases.
- Your blood pressure rises.
- Blood flow is diverted from the digestive system to the brain, major organs, and muscles for protection and increased strength and speed.
- Your liver excretes sugar from increased energy.
- Adrenaline, the arousal hormone, is released from the adrenal gland into the blood.
- Your body perspires to cool off from the increased metabolism.
- Breathing becomes rapid and shallow.

After a stressful event is experienced, the body calms down and resumes its normal functions.

The intensity and duration of the threat will determine how long it takes to return to homeostasis. Life-threatening situations demand an intense response. Some very exciting experiences, like skydiving or speedboat racing, will also elicit a strong response. Suspenseful or frightening movies can produce a definite stress response, especially in young children. Afterward, we sigh with relief — this sigh signals that a cooling down process has begun.

Often, however, the demand isn't quickly removed. For whatever reason, our actions don't result in immediate solutions. After an initial phase of alarm, our bodies will try to adapt to the demand, and try to find a way of returning to normal within the framework of the demand. This is the most common way of dealing with environmental stress. If you live near an airport, you try to get used to the noise level. You learn to adjust to increased noise because you can't change the environment to suit yourself.

If the body is required to adapt too much in too short a time or for too long a period without relief, a breakdown will occur. This stage can end in disease or death. Extensive wear and tear can affect any of the body's organs or systems. There are three stages that follow a threatening experience: the alarm stage, the resistance stage, and the exhaustion stage.

Selye's research of these stages was published in 1950. His first paper on this work was called the "General Adaptation Syndrome." Physiologically, the General Adaptation Syndrome stimulates the body's defense mechanism against disease or injury so that our chances for survival are increased.

As Dr. Kenneth R. Pelletier, author and clinical psychologist at the Psychosomatic Medicine Clinic, Berkeley, California, states in *Mind as Healer, Mind as Slayer:* "Stress disorders are based upon the slow developmental accumulation of psychological and physical stress responses throughout the life of the individual."[3] The unrelieved stress we have experienced since childhood will have an effect on our bodies; wherever our bodies are weakest, we will experience deterioration or disease or both.

The following is a list of disorders which are often stress related.

- tension headache, back pain, muscle cramps or spasm
- neck and shoulder pain, jaw pain, arthritis
- migraine headache, cold hands and feet
- high blood pressure, irregular heart rate, stroke
- heavy perspiration, asthma, breathing problems
- stomach pain, digestive disorders, diarrhea
- abdominal disorders, constipation, allergies
- anxiety, frequent colds, infectious diseases
- skin problems, cancer (some forms)
- hypoglycemia (a decrease in blood sugar)
- hypo- or hyperthyroidism (a rapid heart rate and high blood pressure, or a loss of strength)
- insomnia, fatigue, depression
- overeating or overdieting, alcohol or other drug abuse
- sexual dysfunction, emotional instability
- fears and phobias, some learning disabilities

In addition, chronic pain, whatever the source, is often stress related. Pain clinics across the country teach various relaxation techniques together with medical programs to help patients deal with pain.

Part of the problem with changing our patterns of behavior is the feeling that if we're not experiencing disease now, we won't in the future. It will happen to the other person, we think, not to me. This blocks change. We are all at risk, but when we're not in pain, the risk doesn't seem that great.

Our society reinforces the notion that pain should be blocked out. We are constantly being urged to use alcohol or other drugs to remove whatever distresses us. We are seldom asked to examine the causes of pain in a constructive way. Just get rid of it fast! Never mind that drugs might do us more harm than good. Unfortunately, there is always a price to pay for blocking pain, and the price may be addiction.

Suppose you are treated for chronic back pain with powerful pain-killers. Instead of developing a plan to ease the pain through therapy and relaxation techniques, you become dependent on the drugs. At some point, you will find yourself managing two very difficult problems: chronic pain and addiction to painkillers.

People react to pain in different ways. Some of us realize the problem quickly. Have I been taking care of myself? Getting enough rest? Eating balanced meals, getting exercise? Have I been putting in too many hours at work? Are my family relations satisfying? What is the source of the problem? If the solution isn't easy to implement, it's time to get the proper help whether it's from a doctor, a counselor, or a friend. Some people will pick up the phone the minute it's clear they need help. Some will put it off until they are convinced of the seriousness. Others will stick their heads in the sand, or will keep taking drugs or drinking booze, and ignore it.

People who have pain and medicate it without examining where it comes from may be unwilling to be sensitive to themselves. So, they need more pain to find the motivation to change. For addicts, the recognition that they are no longer in control of their lives may be the turning point. For people with other chronic diseases, a similar realization often occurs. When we realize we can no longer make it alone, we can then face the pain. We need to acknowledge and embrace pain, to see it as a true friend and work with it.

Pain has a function to help us — it can keep us from dying early. This may be a strange concept, but think about it in another context:

Many pregnant women take classes to manage the pain of birth without anesthesia. They learn breathing and muscle control techniques to facilitate the birth of their children. Pain becomes a factor to work with and to learn from. The same can be true in other situations.

Illnesses that interfere with our daily lives in the form of upset stomachs or tension headaches, as well as illnesses that put us in the hospital, always seem like bad news. For people who are busy, even a few days off work with the flu is an unwelcome intrusion. But another side to illness is that it allows us to take the time to rest, reassess, and reaffirm certain aspects of our lives.

Illness may be a way of avoiding other pain. It may be a way to be cared for, to get support from family and friends — support that we may be craving but feel uneasy requesting. It may be a way to get out of relationships that are unsatisfying. It may be a way to get some sleep and slow down when we haven't been taking care of ourselves. Illness gives us permission to change.

But illness can give us excuses for not changing. If the role of the invalid is a comfortable one, we may not be very motivated to get well. Unfortunately, illness is a high price to pay for attention. There are better ways of handling frustration, anger, grief, and guilt. Our bodies shouldn't have to do that work, but too often they do.

If you are in recovery from an addiction, you have already decided that you want to be healthy. You already know how much it costs in terms of your well-being to be addicted, and you're willing to face the pain. Let's take a moment to review your overall health. The Wellness Continuum is a simple graph that gives you an idea of your risk for illness.

WELLNESS CONTINUUM

Perfect Health	+ 2	+ 1	0	− 1	− 2	Death

+ 2 = Excellent
+ 1 = Good
    0 = Fair (neither good nor poor)
− 1 = Poor
− 2 = Serious Illness

On the far left of the graph there's "Perfect Health" and on the far right, "Death." In the middle is a point representing neither health nor illness. Consider your health for the past year. How many illnesses requiring a physician's care did you have? How rundown would you consider yourself now? If a family member or co-worker came down with a cold or flu today, how soon do you think you'd get it? Or would you? Make a note of where you place yourself on the Continuum. We'll come back to it later.

The Social Readjustment Scale

An indicator of how stress affects our health is the Holmes and Rahe Social Readjustment Rating Scale. Dr. Thomas Holmes and Dr. Richard Rahe did their research at the University of Washington's School of Medicine in the 1950s and 1960s. They conducted more than 5,000 interviews to try and link major life events with illnesses or injuries. This scale assigns a number of stress points to events all of us are likely to encounter. The most stressful, the death of a spouse, receives the highest number of points; a minor violation of the law receives the least. Notice that marriage, outstanding personal achievement, and a vacation are included. Though we may not think of these events as stressful, they all require adaptation and change. Looking back over the past year, which of these events did you experience? When you've finished, total your number of points.

HOLMES AND RAHE SOCIAL READJUSTMENT RATING SCALE

EVENT	VALUE
Death of a spouse	100
Divorce	73
Marital separation	65
Jail term	63
Death of close family member	63
Personal injury or illness	53
Marriage	50
Fired at work	47
Marital reconciliation	45

EVENT	VALUE
Retirement	45
Change in health of family member	45
Pregnancy	40
Sex difficulties	39
Gain of new family member	39
Business readjustment	39
Change in financial state	38
Death of close friend	37
Change to different line of work	36
Change in number of arguments with spouse	35
Mortgage of $10,000	31
Foreclosure of mortgage or loan	30
Change in responsibilities at work	29
Son or daughter leaving home	29
Trouble with in-laws	29
Outstanding personal achievement	28
Spouse begins or stops work	26
Begin or end school	26
Change in living conditions	25
Revision of personal habits	24
Trouble with boss	23
Change in work hours or conditions	20
Change in residence	20
Change in schools	20
Change in church activities	19
Change in social activities	18
Mortgage or loan less than $10,000	17
Change in sleeping habits	16
Change in number of family get-togethers	15
Change in eating habits	15
Vacation	13
Christmas	12
Minor violation of the law	11
TOTAL	

Reprinted with permission from Journal of Psychosomatic Research, *Volume II, Dr. Thomas Holmes and Dr. Richard Rahe, copyright 1967, Pergamon Journals, Ltd.*

You'll notice that one major change, such as retirement, brings along with it other changes, such as a change in financial status, change in work responsibilities, and change in living conditions. Therefore, a major change is never isolated. As you can see, the stressful events listed in this scale are environmental, social, physical, and psychological. Holmes and Rahe calculated that a person with 150 stress points for the past year has a 50-50 chance of getting ill. A person with 300 stress points for the past year will almost certainly become ill.

Of course, not everyone will fit this prediction. Some people with few stress points may experience illness on a frequent basis possibly due to underlying stressors (such as chemical dependency, lack of personal support, or poor self-esteem that causes anxiety). Other people with a high number of stress points may not become ill because they are given personal support and feel confident about themselves. Each of us has a unique set of factors that work for or against us.

A woman who has experienced the trauma of her husband's death may, in the first year, catch a cold or the flu more often than she ever has in her life. A weekend trip may prove unusually exhausting because of the high level of adapting she is required to do on a daily basis. It is especially important for her to control the changes in her life as much as possible. For instance, it would not be good for her to change residences if she doesn't have to.

A normal stress reaction will occur when the threat is clearly identified. It's when the threat is prolonged or ambiguous, or when several kinds of stress exist at once that the person is at greater risk to become ill. As a starting point for awareness, look at your total number of points on the Social Readjustment Rating Scale and go back to the Wellness Continuum. The additional information provided by the scale may have altered your perception of where you stand on the continuum. Take another look: were you right about your position the first time? Have you moved closer to either end?

Positive change is possible when you know where you stand right now. It has taken years — maybe all your life — to produce your reactions to stress. It will take time and help to change them.

CHAPTER 2

Hostility

This is a self-quiz on anger. Answer the following questions by circling the letter which best describes your behavior: A = always; S = sometimes; and R = rarely.

1. Do you become irritated when you experience unexpected delays?   A   S   R
2. Do you consider yourself an aggressive driver?   A   S   R
3. Do you become angry when someone passes you on the road?   A   S   R
4. Does waiting in line annoy you?   A   S   R
5. Do you tend to finish your meals before others do?   A   S   R
6. Do you tend to hurry the speech of others?   A   S   R
7. Do you schedule more and more activities in less and less time?   A   S   R
8. Have others told you that you talk, walk, or eat too fast?   A   S   R
9. Do you feel guilty or uncomfortable when it's time to relax?   A   S   R
10. Are you afraid to slow down?   A   S   R
11. When you have conversations, do you have trouble listening to others?   A   S   R

12. Do you feel you have more responsibility than others at work?   A   S   R

13. Do you often feel pressured?   A   S   R

14. Do you tend to do or think about several things at once (for example, sorting out the mail while talking on the phone, or reading while watching television)?   A   S   R

15. Do you tend to be unaware of your environment, the weather, or what people are wearing?   A   S   R

16. Do you feel antagonistic toward your peers at work, and believe that you do a better job than they do?   A   S   R

17. Is it difficult for you to "turn off" your competitiveness?   A   S   R

18. Do you acknowledge that you are pressed for time, frequently angry, and highly competitive, but that this behavior is best for you and will have no ill effects?   A   S   R

19. Do you notice that others avoid dealing with you?   A   S   R

20. Do you find your thoughts are critical of yourself and others (filled with words like "stupid," "idiot," and "dumb")?   A   S   R

21. Do you minimize the need for support or calling a sponsor or friend, thinking you should know the answers and don't need help as much as others?   A   S   R

22. Do you find yourself complaining a lot and others are giving you advice that you resent?   A   S   R

23. Do you need to get your way without consideration of others, thinking you know what's best in the situation?   A   S   R

24. At meetings do you evaluate the leaders and formulate a plan for how they could have been better?   A   S   R

Give yourself three points for every "A" you have circled, two points for every "S," and one point for every "R." Total your score. If your total is less than 36, hostility probably is not a major issue for you. If your range is 37 to 60, hostility is definitely a concern that is affecting other areas of your life. If your score is 61 to 72, hostility is a major issue; your anger is affecting most areas of your life. You can benefit from understanding your pattern of anger and identifying areas you can change.

Anger is one of the toughest issues to deal with in recovery. Addicts were often angry while they were using, but the alcohol or other drugs helped numb the pain. For the family, a great deal of anger surrounded the user. Once in recovery, this anger must be dealt with in order to get rid of it. Anger and resentment aren't always simple to recognize because denial plays such an important role in coping with feelings.

Anger can be expressed through violence, depression, manipulation, compulsive eating, vandalism, suicide, and other negative behaviors. The way we choose to express anger is often related to what is accepted in the family. If an addict is unpredictably violent when drunk or high, the spouse may never raise his or her voice. When the spouse is angry, he or she may overeat and become depressed. Managing anger in this way greatly adds to the unpredictability and instability of life. When we feel that chaos is all we can expect, we feel powerless and anxious — and angry.

Once in recovery, through counseling and support group involvement, both the addict and the family may feel strange or even frightened of the anger they feel. The development of skills to cope with anger positively takes time and practice. While they learn to deal with the anger that arises in the normal course of living, they are also challenged by the need to face the resentments that have built up over a lifetime. That's why there's an important recovery philosophy in coping "one day at a time."

Anger is a normal emotion: it happens to everyone. Its purpose is to provide us with the energy we need in order to act appropriately at difficult times. It always has an object — we're angry at something or someone. When we communicate our anger, we let others know how we feel and that our feelings are to be taken seriously. When we feel angry, we have to do something with those feelings. If we turn them on ourselves, we become depressed, and feel guilty and help-less. If we choose to communicate our feelings to others, we can do it in positive and negative ways.

In other words, if we deal with anger positively, in an assertive manner, we get rid of anger and enhance our self-esteem. If we communicate anger negatively and become abusive, we complicate the situation and bring guilt, pain, and more anger back to ourselves. Violence, whether physical or psychological, is never appropriate. Yet, in addictive homes, anger is often expressed in extreme ways through violence, psychological abuse, neglect, or abandonment.

Not expressing our anger can have deadly consequences: it can lead to a number of diseases which are thought to be stress-related, including high blood pressure, ulcers, and cancer. The recovering person should always express anger in safe surroundings because of the tendency to overreact. Because we know there will be times when we are angry, we can plan for them when we're feeling happy.

Types of Anger

Anger is such a frightening emotion that some people build their whole lives around avoiding or suppressing it.

There are people who channel their anger into excessive competitiveness. They have an overwhelming need to succeed, whatever the cost, and they bristle with hostile energy.

There are people who are always there for us, and who go to great extremes to avoid conflict — so much so that they seldom or never discuss their feelings, so it's difficult to know what's going on with them.

There are people who act as victims, and see the world as totally unfair. They are extremely insecure and will not express anger directly, but use guilt to get what they want. For example, they may pretend to be ill so their mate will do the housework.

There are also people who refuse to accept responsibility and leave problems to others, while they have a good time. These people have no empathy for others — they are immature — and are best known for creating chaos.

Our families, because they are so familiar to us, bear the brunt of our anger — whether the anger is expressed as uncontrolled rage or manipulative behavior. Living in the same house provides ample opportunity to lash out, and daily contact allows irritation to grow. We may want our families to change and they may fight it; or our families may want us to change, and we resent it.

Hostility and Type A Behavior

People who act as though they live in a hostile world and are always ready for battle, can often be diagnosed as having the Type A behavior syndrome, which was first identified in the early sixties by cardiologists Meyer Friedman and Ray H. Rosenman. Friedman and Rosenman explain how to recognize the Type A pattern in yourself, how and why Type A behavior leads to heart disease, and what you can do if you are a Type A. In their book, *Type A Behavior and Your Heart*, the authors found that heart attack patients frequently exhibited three distinct traits: insecurity, time urgency, and hostility. These people feel they need to get more and more done in less and less time: their lives are characterized by struggle. Because of this, their bodies are constantly engaged in the fight or flight response. Their hearts work extra hard, and, as a natural consequence, their bodies may produce larger quantities of cholesterol. Both the Type A behavior and excess cholesterol have been identified as factors in the development of heart disease.[1]

These people, like addicts, don't deal with their anger constructively, but use denial to cope with it. They seldom recognize they are angry, and they express hostility in virtually every action. Anyone or anything that obstructs or appears to obstruct them receives a message loud and clear: get out of my way! They perceive other people as acting in threatening ways even in the most mundane circumstances, such as while driving or standing in the check-out line or playing tennis. Because being rushed for time is a way of life for the Type A person, he or she will frequently finish others' sentences for them, fiddle, twitch, or move incessantly.[2]

Type A's tend to be very success oriented. They are dedicated to their jobs, and frequently work compulsively. They are poor listeners and have trouble delegating tasks because they believe only they can "do it right." At the base of this behavior is low self-esteem. The Type A person has profound doubts about his or her self-worth. This is why success, wealth, and prestige mean so much. Unfortunately, Type A's receive a great deal of support from our society, because we regard success so highly. Just as the addict lives a life out of control, the Type A lives a life characterized by tunnel vision — and the tunnel is full of hostility.

Type A behavior is not the same as stress, though it is a particularly stressful way to behave. The syndrome is a style of reaction, a framework for reaction to stress, and it creates stress for others. As Friedman and Rosenman state, "*Type A Behavior* is not a psychosis or a complex of worries or fears or phobias or obsessions, but a socially acceptable — indeed often praised — form of conflict."[3]

People who possess Type B traits, on the other hand, have a very different view of life; time is not their enemy, and the world is not a hostile place. These people operate from a fundamental core of self-worth that enables them to meet challenges in an objective, creative manner. They may be just as ambitious and successful as Type A's, but their methods are different. Type B people are frequently good listeners who rely on their associates for information and solutions — they are team players. Balance characterizes their lives.[4]

Both Type A and Type B behavior is learned. It is possible to replace the more self-destructive Type A traits with the life-enhancing Type B's. The basis of change is self-awareness. On an emotional level, the Type A person must go into recovery in a similar way as the addict; both must learn to cope with their feelings in healthy ways.

Aggressive, Passive, and Assertive Behavior

People who do not perceive their emotions rationally, who are in denial about them, or who overreact to situations, are unable to tell the difference between aggressive, passive, and assertive behavior, and thus can't choose the response that is appropriate.

Aggressive behavior is an overheated way to communicate. Emotions are out of control: people shout, pound on the table or other people, and say things they don't mean but are hurtful to others.

There is no discussion, no dialogue, and no way to work out a solution that will yield satisfaction to either party. The people who act aggressively often believe others should be able to read their minds. "Anyone with a brain would know I hate that kind of music!" Rages are frequently followed by periods of guilt and promises of reform that aren't realistic. Pent-up anger will seek an opening, and aggressive behavior is a common one.

Passive behavior is equally common. Deep insecurity keeps passive people from wanting to "rock the boat" with their anger. When situations cause problems for passive people, they repress their feelings, say nothing, and pretend everything is all right. People who are Type A often behave passively, especially regarding the requests of others. In this way, the requests are frozen in a perpetual "Of course I will" response.

Passive people fear conflict because they think conflict means they are not good people. In addictive homes, the spouse or children may display passive behavior as an antidote to the chaos. People who display passive behavior also believe others should know how they feel. "Why would you ask me to do that for you when you know how busy I already am?" Unable to set limits, the passive person allows others to do so and is frequently resentful of it.

Unlike passive or aggressive responses, the assertive response is an open and direct method of communication where emotions are expressed in positive ways. Assertive responses are under control because we accept them as valid and important. We are not threatened by these responses. Thus, they are neither overheated nor frozen responses. In difficult situations, an assertive response allows the person on the receiving end to enter into a solution of mutual benefit to both parties. Whether or not a favorable outcome can be reached, we have at least expressed ourselves in a positive way and have maintained self-esteem. Learning assertive skills is an important goal in recovery from stress-producing behavior. It requires self-awareness, self-assessment, good communication skills, and planning.

Dealing with Anger

Suppose you are in a restaurant, having lunch with a new friend. You have about an hour to eat, and you hope to make this a pleasant experience for your friend. Your waiter is slow in taking your order, and your food is late. Instead of a relaxed and congenial meal, you are forced to eat very quickly. This makes you uncomfortable. How would you handle this situation?

1. Protest strongly to the waiter, the cashier, and other diners about the "lousy service, the disgraceful treatment, and the inconvenience" this has caused you. You demand to see the manager, and tell her that the waiter should be fired if she wants to keep any customers at all.
2. Say nothing to the waiter, pay your bill, and leave the restaurant, fuming and vowing "never to go there again!"
3. Express your dissatisfaction to the waiter in a direct but controlled manner. He apologizes and explains that an emergency has left the restaurant short-staffed. As a conciliatory measure, he does not charge you for your beverages. You accept this as recompense.

Suppose you have planned a surprise dinner for your husband's 60th day of sobriety. He left at 5:00 P.M. to attend an Alcoholics Anonymous meeting — the tenth A.A. meeting he has been to this week. It's now 12:30 A.M. and he just arrived home, filled with enthusiasm about some wonderful people he met at the meeting. He explains that everyone went to the coffee shop afterward and "time sure passed quickly." Meanwhile, you've been sitting at home with a spoiled dinner and spoiled plans for a romantic evening. What would you do?

1. Yell at him. Tell him that you had plans and he ruined them. Make sure he knows how worried you were that something happened to him.
2. Say, "That's okay dear. I'm happy for you" through clenched teeth, and then march off to bed.
3. Express that you were concerned about his coming home so late. Ask him to call you from now on when he'll be later than usual. Assure him that his sobriety is very important to

you, but so is your marriage. Make plans to spend some time alone together.

The following technique on owning feelings can improve self-awareness. This technique helps us to use language to express what we really feel and mean, instead of filtering the language through denial to make it more acceptable. We can disavow our feelings by putting them somewhere else. This technique requires that you listen to yourself and to others. We tend to displace our feelings in especially emotional or threatening situations — such as when we're angry — but it can be so pervasive that we no longer "own" anything we feel.

First, we'll give you some common examples of statements as well as the feelings these statements represent. Next, you can make a note of some comments you make, and what feelings they represent. Do this with family members or friends; or, if you're recovering from an addiction, do this with your peers in recovery so that you're not working in a vacuum and your statements accurately reflect your actual behavior. Once you are familiar with this technique, practice "owning" your feelings with others in nonthreatening situations. In this way, you'll learn to build an important skill.

STATEMENTS WE MAKE	HOW WE OWN OUR FEELINGS AND NEEDS
1. That was scary!	I was frightened!
2. You make me so angry!	I am angry with you!
3. That was a lousy meal.	I didn't like the food.
4. Let's go home.	I want to go home.

MORE STATEMENTS WE MAKE	YOU FILL IN THE FEELINGS
1. He's a creep!	I . . .
2. Don't do that to me!	I . . .
3. That coat looks good on you.	I . . .
4. You make me so happy!	I . . .

OUR COMMON STATEMENTS   WHAT YOU REALLY MEAN

1.

2.

3.

4.

Communication Skills

The following is a list from *Learning to Live Again* by Terrence Gorski, Merlene Miller, and David Miller. These are the characteristics of good communicators:

1. They are good listeners. It is often true that the main ingredient in good communication is careful listening.
2. They help those speaking to them to be complete and accurate by giving them verbal and nonverbal encouragement while listening.
3. They do not dominate the discussion. There is sensitivity to the other person or persons in the conversation.
4. They give total attention to what is being said, rather than thinking about how they will answer what is being said.
5. They express themselves in ways meant to send meaning accurately to the others in a conversation, rather than to impress listeners with how smart they are.[5]

Listening is a skill worth developing. However, there are also times when we need to confront someone about his or her behavior. Confrontation is not the same as fighting — it's presenting your feelings about the subject in a nonthreatening way and allowing the other person to do the same. This is the way solutions are found that mutually benefit all people involved. Confrontations may not always end in getting what we want (that may not be realistic), but they do end in the satisfaction of having handled our feelings appropriately. When we choose this approach, our feelings are under our control. Our stress level is manageable because our feelings are manageable. We can practice these skills by role playing with others in nonthreatening situations.

Confrontation Skills
Gayle Rosellini and Mark Worden, in their book, *Of Course You're Angry*, list these confrontation skills for recovering from stressful behavior.

- Pick a good time and place.
- Be serious and firm, but loving.
- State your concerns clearly and immediately. ("I feel. . . . ")
- Use specific examples.
- Use *I* statements versus *you* statements.
- Stay on track.
- Use rational self-talk to stay calm and reasonable.
- Present clear, reasonable, and positive solutions.
- State your commitment to solve the problem.
- Don't insist on 100% acquiescence to your every wish.
- Show your appreciation for cooperation.[6]

When you feel yourself tensing up, take a deep breath and slow down. Remind yourself that anger is normal; overreaction is a choice that leads to more stress as well as guilt and depression. If you feel yourself about to blowup, take yourself out of the discussion until you are in control and ready to resume.

Techniques for Calming Others
With so much pressure and tension everywhere, there are ways we can prevent conflict by calming others.

- Model calmness.
- Listen openly and sympathetically.
- Reassure the other person.
- Help save face.[7]

There will be a time when you will be on the receiving end of someone else's anger. Remember that you can choose your reaction, and it doesn't have to be rage or tears. By truly listening to the other person and responding honestly without accusations or judgments, you'll be able to reach a positive conclusion. Anger is a strong emotion. It should be respected.

Seeking Professional Help

Much of the work required in the process of coping with anger in positive ways needs to be done under the guidance of professional counselors. The therapist's job is to sift through our defenses and self-destructive patterns and to help us know ourselves better. A therapist can be very helpful in a time of crisis, and can also be an excellent resource over a long period of time. When you're learning new coping skills, a therapist can help you attain your goals.

There are many types of therapy. If you have a chronic disease such as alcoholism, you may want to talk with someone who has counseling experience in that field. Or you may want to talk with a professional who reflects your religious or philosophical values. Or you may want someone to help you through a particular crisis such as death or divorce. Listed here are some of the guidelines for selecting professional help from *The Road Less Traveled* by M. Scott Peck.[8]

1. Psychotherapy is a major investment in your time and money. Shop around for someone you are comfortable with.
2. Ask questions to find out what the therapist's orientation is. Are you comfortable with that?
3. Is he or she a genuinely caring person? This is more important than the credentials on the wall.
4. Ask your friends for recommendations. Word of mouth is usually the best way to find a therapist.

Most hospitals have social workers, psychologists, psychiatrists, and ministers, priests, and rabbis on staff, any of whom could make informed recommendations.

Asking for help is not a sign of weakness. It is, in fact, a sign of strength. It is a step toward growth, and necessary for recovery from stressful behavior.

CHAPTER 3

Grief

Change is inevitable. From infancy to death we are faced with a series of changes, each with its own challenges and rewards. When we move from one phase of our lives to another, sometimes we're ready and sometimes we're not. We're more likely to feel the loss of what has passed when we aren't ready for change. This is the time for grief. We grieve when we are separated from someone or something we love, sometimes forever.

In order to get on with our lives, we must work through the pain of loss, which is often called *grief work.* Failure to do grief work can have serious repercussions. Most recovering people are aware of the high price they will pay if they avoid feelings of depression, anger, and guilt.

The death of a loved one is the most severe loss we can face in life. This experience, however, is inevitable. There are a number of factors involved in how severe the trauma will be, but ultimately we all face a devastating loss. The death of a young person may be overwhelmingly tragic, especially to parents. After all, when children are unable to live out their lives, expectations are disrupted. Nevertheless, a man who has just buried his wife of 50 years may grieve just as hard because he had a whole lifetime with someone he loved.

Death is only one experience that causes grief. Divorce also involves substantial loss. The Holmes and Rahe Social Readjustment Rating Scale ranks divorce as the second most stressful event. Many of the other categories in the scale involve loss as well: the loss of a job, home, or financial security. Grief can likewise accompany other situations: leaving good friends to take a new job, children going off to college, and retiring. These are major changes that are stressful and involve loss.

We become familiar with the grief process as children. When a special friend moves away or a pet dies, we lose a cherished part of our world. Even at that young age we go through an entire grief process before we move on to establish new relationships. In early adolescence we seek to grow up as fast as we can while still needing the protection of childhood. Loss due to transitions follow us throughout life.

There are also losses that affect us as a global community. Certain situations, such as war, involve all of us. Many Americans who lived through the Vietnam conflict suffered losses, directly or indirectly, of self-esteem and idealism. The current AIDS epidemic is an example of loss on a global level: many people have died from a disease that has no cure. Despite the fact that we may not grieve over these issues, they can affect the way we see ourselves.

Part of loss is external: a job, a spouse, or a best friend. Part of loss is internal: how we feel about ourselves after a significant part of our lives is gone. Feelings of insecurity and helplessness are common. The grief process is upsetting, painful, and, if we have never examined what goes on, surprising.

Our culture provides few traditions for us as we grieve. Typically, when there's a death in the family, our relatives and friends gather around during the first difficult days to help out. The funeral or memorial services enable us to express our sorrow as a group, though we much prefer restraint to tears despite how difficult that can be. The first few weeks following the death of a loved one, families are left pretty much on their own when it comes to rebuilding their lives. If time is our only measure, when are we supposed to be healed?

For many people divorce is nearly as traumatic as death, yet there are even fewer rules to follow. Are we supposed to feel good? Some people encourage us to celebrate — should we? If our children live with our previous partner, how do we treat them? These are questions that provoke strong feelings, and it isn't obvious where we can go with these feelings. For people who abuse alcohol or other drugs, the tendency is to obliterate the feelings. It doesn't work. The only way through the pain is to experience it and to let it go.

The Grief Process

We begin the acute phase of the grief process by going into shock. This is a form of protection from pain during the first few days. We feel numb; nothing much penetrates. We may wander around, saying, "I can't believe it!" We have suffered a tremendous blow, and our bodies will respond with interrupted sleep, temporary loss of memory, or perhaps the inability to complete simple tasks. We aren't as capable of thinking things through. This is a time for others to fill in for us with both the routine responsibilities of life as well as the extraordinary requirements of the situation. We may not even be able to cry at this point.

"Acting Out" Pain

As the shock begins to wear off, instead of facing the reality of the pain, it is possible to relieve the pain by drinking, taking other drugs, overeating, or gambling. The shock seems preferable to the pain, so some people choose to remain numb. The tendency may be to skip over the depression and the rest of the stages in the grief process, and use statements like, "I'm fine, really. Everything's okay." This, however, is a lie. It is normal to experience some denial, but there is a difference between the temporary methods of relief in this phase and the more serious chronic methods that become a lifestyle.

Depression: Anger, Guilt, Bargaining

For those of us who overcome denial, and when the shock starts to wear off, we begin to cry. Now we feel the brunt of our loss, and it hurts. Crying is a healthy release for pain; both men and women need to cry. We become depressed. It's common to become preoccupied with the deceased, to daydream about him or her, and to mistake others for that person. We might question our sanity at this point; the visions seem so real. We feel sluggish, tired, and lost. Our eating and sleeping habits are disrupted. We have trouble coping.

We may not have trouble getting angry, especially at those who might have had some role in our loss: the hospital staff, physicians, clergy, lawyers, funeral directors, or insurance agents. We might think: *It's all their fault!* We're suffering for the incompetency of others, and why? Our lives have been turned upside down. We think there's no relief in sight — even a fool can see who's to blame. If we get no satisfaction by yelling at our debtors, we may show hostility by driving recklessly or taking other physical risks.

Anger is a way of coping with the depression. It is comforting to have that release even though it's not a substitute for the pain. This type of anger is not the same as we experience later in the grieving process. Here our anger serves to help us get through the first difficult stage. Our anger is generally unfocused — we are angry at everyone and everything.

Another common reaction is guilt. "If only I'd been there," we say. The tendency is to want to find ways to avoid the pain, and the "what if" game is very handy. An alcoholic, for example, may drag herself deeper into the abyss by blaming herself for her husband's departure. She thinks she is worthless, and this is even more reason to drink. When she is drunk, she feels numb. Every time she sobers up, however, she begins to hurt again, and instead of acknowledging it, she plays the "what if" game until she can't stand it and starts to drink.

Illnesses are common at this time, although they are likely to occur anytime during the grief process. We can even end up in the hospital dealing with yet another loss — the loss of health. Illness is often the chance for us to rest and to receive attention and care from others. Illness can also be an excuse not to face the primary pain — the grief — for various periods of time.

As we move on into the depression phase, we are tempted to bargain with God to minimize the pain. We want to make a deal to make things all right again. "I promise to stay sober forever if you'll let my family come back," or, "If you'll just take this pain away, I'll never do another bad thing." We're trying to get back some control, which is normal, but the way we go about it leads to a dead end — most of our bargains are unrealistic. When we don't live up to the promises made in desperation, we set ourselves up for more grief and depression.

Another wave of anger will then occur, perhaps because our bargaining doesn't pay off. This phase is an important one because we are now angry at the person (or thing) that left us. This seems irrational in the case of death, since few of us choose to die. But the anger is real. When we love someone very much, we invest a great deal in him or her: time, energy, hope, effort, and self-esteem. When that person dies, he or she has gone off with our investment, as if our life savings had been taken in a bank robbery. Wouldn't we be angry at a thief who stole our treasures? Well, here someone has gone off with our emotional savings. We may not consciously think of it quite this way when a person we love passes away, but we might feel this anger in our hearts — and it's normal to do so.

An interesting thing happens when we face up to this anger: it begins to lose its power. We might attack a punching bag, throw rocks in a lake, or yell at the top of our lungs. At that point, when we feel angry and know we're angry at the person we loved, there is catharsis, a purging that is a release from tension.

After we have gone through the anger, we begin to put things back together. This means that we can now rebuild our lives without the person we loved. It's like turning the last page of a book. We can look back over our lives and reread the events that led up to the loss, the loss itself, and the difficult aftermath. Now, however, there is a feeling of acceptance and completion. We can move on. All of those feelings in the grief process that were so turbulent, demanding, and fractured, are integrated because we chose to face them, not avoid them. The anger, guilt, and depression become positive, and growth takes place.

The lessons we learn in the grief process are lessons for managing stress, and dealing with future losses. We learn that acute grief causes tremendous upheaval, and that it takes time to recover from the loss. During this time we must be willing to face our feelings of guilt, anger, depression, and pain in a responsible, positive way. If we don't resolve our feelings, they stay with us, coloring every aspect of our lives and placing undue stress on new relationships.

There are times when events or people will trigger "mini" depressions. Anniversaries are particularly difficult, and can result in "anniversary depression." A year or so after the death of a loved one or after a divorce, we may be susceptible to illness, accidents, or erratic behavior. Binges are often associated with the anniversary of a loss. This indicates that there are some unfinished emotions to deal with. Knowing this, we can make plans for these anniversaries that will reduce the intensity of the pain. For example, we might spend time with loving friends who will listen to our worries and fears, yet help us focus on the positive aspects of our present lives.

The Grief Cycle

Although no one can set an absolute time frame for a grief cycle, there is general agreement that anything less than a year to eighteen months for grieving the death of a spouse is probably not long enough. There are a number of factors that affect the length of this period.

- Who was the person in your life? The closer the relationship, the greater the loss will be.
- What was the nature of your relationship? The strengths and weaknesses of the relationship are important as well. While nearly all couples and families have unresolved conflicts, the number and severity of these conflicts can greatly affect the grieving process. In the case of a terminally ill person, the family may be burdened by hospital bills. Families often quarrel over the will or possessions when they're really angry at the person who died. Issues still unsettled at the time of death will complicate the grieving process.
- How did the person die? Was death due to old age, an accident, suicide, or homicide? Was the family able to say goodbye? These things make a difference to the bereaved. Violent death, especially homicide, brings with it difficult issues such as revenge, and will increase the guilt ("Why couldn't I protect her?"). If justice isn't done, the process is harder because the resolution of the conflict is left up to the bereaved. A suicide carries tremendous consequences as well, primarily guilt and social stigma.

- How were you brought up to cope with loss? The lessons you learned as a child will greatly influence how you handle grief as an adult. If, when you were growing up, feelings were not freely expressed and family members did not rely on one another for support, you'll probably not feel like doing so. Avoiding your own emotions will hamper your grief work.
- What is your belief system? Often people find comfort and strength in their grief work if they have faith in God or a Higher Power. Belief in an afterlife or eternal cycle of renewal and rebirth helps some people deal with pain. This process utilizes the power of hope to heal. The belief that the deceased is part of a timeless unity gives us a sense of serenity.
- How strong is your social network? Are there relatives and friends who can support you during this process? Can you call on professionals — therapists, counselors, clergy — to get you through the rough spots? Are there people who can fill in for you at work or home? The stronger the network, and the better we are at asking for help when we need it, the easier the grieving will be.

Recovery and Grief

For the recovering person, the loss of the addictive substance can be a very serious loss. Consider what alcohol has done for the alcoholic: it has been a barrier against pain, guilt, and anger. Although an alcoholic has never been able to progress in her grief work, she has escaped from reality. She has been able to believe that she was in control and everything was fine, even though it wasn't. When she gives up alcohol, however, she not only loses her good friend, but now must face the pain she tried so hard to avoid. There's nothing to protect her from it anymore. (Oftentimes the grief process doesn't get started until several months following sobriety.) Her first anniversary of being sober may not cause her much joy: she may be so angry she can't see straight, or so depressed she doesn't want to. Alcohol had been a big "investment"; now it's a big loss.

After facing this problem, it is necessary to also face the unresolved grief from the past. Unresolved grief, also called *chronic grief,* can cause us to make decisions in our lives that are not in our best interest.

For example, a boy who is not encouraged to do his grief work after the death of his father may have difficulties forming close relationships as an adult. The sorrow, anger, and guilt he felt as a child remains bottled up inside. He fears a loss, and has equated love with loss. Thus, he chooses to avoid involvement with others despite its potential for personal growth and happiness.

Dealing with chronic grief might be the hardest work we'll ever do. It is said that active alcoholics are in a state of constant, unresolved grief. When we choose sobriety, we also choose to face our losses.

Negative Ways of Expressing Grief

There are a number of ways we act out our grief during the depression phase. One very common way is sexually, when we see our release from pain in starting a new relationship. The process of getting involved with someone new is a powerful diversion. The feelings are pleasant, and what a relief! Instead of doing our grief work, we choose to fall in love — often obsessively. The new relationship seems the answer to all our prayers: we feel alive again. Unfortunately, what we are doing is simply setting ourselves up for failure. Things are fine for a while, and then reality begins to creep into our new relationship.

We find ourselves bringing unresolved feelings into our new, "perfect" relationship. The new relationship doesn't stand much of a chance, being under the strain of both the past and present. In the worst situation, the relationship ends, and we have yet another serious loss on our hands — thus, more grief. This pattern can repeat itself many times unless we face our pain.

Overwork is also another way of acting out grief. We can go into the office and prove we're fine by working harder and longer than anybody else. The old adage about work keeping our minds off our grief is only valid up to a point. If it takes the place of our grief, we aren't dealing with our feelings, but hiding from them. Being caught up in our work delays that inevitable time when we will be alone with our depression.

We can get caught in the trap of self-pity, which is a way of showing anger without acknowledging we are angry. We are like a broken record, telling everyone how hard we've had it. "Life's a bitch and then you die." It's easy to get stuck here, for there are many people who are receptive to our complaints. It's easier to complain than it is to act. It's harder to turn those feelings around into something positive than to nurse the negative feelings *ad infinitum.*

Sometimes we become more and more isolated in our grief, choosing not to share it with anyone else, even trusted friends. This often results in prolonged depression when even the tasks of ordinary living are too difficult. It is a period of disorganization and emotional turmoil. Personality changes take place. A normally calm person may have angry outbursts, or someone who has always taken charge may seem confused. In families, these changes can be disruptive. Much of the intense stress created during this time is from not knowing and understanding how to cope with change. It can make us frantic.

Children tend to blame themselves for the death of a parent or their parents' divorce. This guilt can follow them into adulthood unless they can face it and work through it. Usually they need a trained therapist to help them. We tend to feel bad or unworthy at some point in our grief work, and if we don't get out of that, we may choose partners or jobs that reinforce this attitude. This leads to breakups or breakdowns and a spiral of self-destruction. We may stay in relationships or jobs that encourage us to feel unworthy because that's what we're used to. The familiar seems much more attractive than change — especially when change is accompanied by pain.

We may harm ourselves by being unwilling or unable to make friends or form close ties of any sort. We may compensate by over-achieving, or marrying a parent replacement (sometimes more than once). Nothing we do, however, seems to alleviate the old doubts, and, in an attempt to avoid this pain, we might turn to alcohol, other drugs, or other addictive behaviors.

When our present lives require so much of us in terms of energy and effort, we're only hindering our success by continuing to behave as if some very old misconceptions are valid. When we see ourselves as unworthy, we're not facing reality.

Harboring losses takes energy and creativity that we could use to enrich our lives. Letting go of grief frees us for the challenges of the present, and helps us relax.

Persistent and generalized hostility, nagging self-doubts, and feelings of guilt, fear, or betrayal can be the result of unresolved grief. Though these feelings are common to all of us at some time or another, their continued influence on our lives is a warning that some issue or event remains unresolved.

As the shock of a significant loss begins to wear off, it is often best to simply allow yourself to recuperate at a pace best suited to your emotional and physical well-being. If this means a longer break from work or family responsibilities, then, if possible, arrange that. If that option isn't available to you, seek professional counseling.

If you are grieving, remember that your reactions are appropriate for you. Your feelings will run the gamut, and this will be exhausting. Allow yourself to express grief, both in tears and anger, and rely on good friends to help and understand. Grieving takes time — don't be in a hurry. Try to realize that grieving is a process, and you *will* make headway. Don't postpone the pain. It won't go away; it's the path to rehabilitation.

Be forgiving of your inadequacies at this time. The blow you have suffered will cause changes in temperament and behavior but they are temporary. Other family members will also experience confusing and conflicting feelings. Don't try to manage the grief of those around you. If a situation arises where a therapist is needed, remember that expert help is a positive move, not a sign of weakness or mental illness.

This is the time to refrain from new challenges if possible. Get plenty of rest and exercise, and eat a balanced diet. Don't skip meals, and stay away from caffeine, nicotine, and sugar as much as possible. Treat your body kindly; nurture yourself, and allow others to help you.

Alcoholics Anonymous supports the philosophy that there is a way to keep a person from drinking: a spiritual awakening — a belief in a Power that is greater than oneself. This brings a new, more positive outlook on life. A spiritual awakening requires support from people who have been through grief and who will tell us the truth.

Counseling is also a good idea if you don't feel comfortable sharing grief with family members or friends. No matter what you're feeling, it's appropriate for you; there is no "right way" to be in pain. If you are caught in addictive behavior, then therapy would certainly be helpful. Few of us can get through the added burden of unresolved past grief on our own.

If you're trying to help a person who has recently lost someone important, realize that his or her behavior may appear abnormal to you, but it's normal for the person to react in such a way to an important loss. This is the time to recognize your own limitations. Your care can be put to use in many ways that will be useful to the person and comfortable for you. Your friend or relative will not be helped knowing that you're headed for a binge or you may break down under the strain. Share your thoughts and feelings among other friends or professionals. Remember that you will feel the loss too. Take care of yourself.

Each of us has a different time frame for grieving. Simply recognizing this is a big help. It takes as long as needed.

As a Chinese proverb says, "The journey of a lifetime begins with but one step."

CHAPTER 4

Relapse

As most of us in recovery have realized, recovery is not a straight line from sobriety to joyful, healthy living. There are times when recovery seems easy, and times when it most definitely is not. These difficult times are times of heavy stress for us and for our families.

The recovery process begins by admitting to ourselves that we are addicted. We must then go through withdrawal when we abstain from our drug of choice. Next comes crisis management where we cope with reality without abusing alcohol or other drugs. After this, we begin to balance our lives and the way we see ourselves and the world. Going from abstinence to comfortable living to productive living leads to healthy growth. Every step in this process must be completed before we go on to another. If we fail to complete certain tasks, we are stuck. When we are stuck, we are at risk for relapse.

Relapse begins much sooner than the point where we resume alcohol or other drug use. First, we become dysfunctional, and then relapse into addictive use to cover the pain. By the time we start drinking or using, we are quite far along in the relapse process.

When we are not actively pursuing a Twelve Step program to improve our lives, we are usually sliding back toward addiction. We have abnormal reactions to our chosen drug while using it; we also have abnormal reactions after we've stopped using it. This is part of the recovery process. These symptoms are called *post acute withdrawal*,[1] and they can occur anytime during recovery. Post acute withdrawal means symptoms that occur after acute withdrawal. Acute withdrawal occurs when we stop using chemicals. Our bodies, which are dependent on chemicals, undergo a series of dramatic changes in order to cope without the drugs. Acute withdrawal usually lasts from one to two weeks, and is then followed by post acute withdrawal. These are symptoms which occur with abstinence. Understanding these symptoms and how to manage them will aid our recovery. The symptoms include difficulty in thinking clearly or diminished concentration or both, impaired memory, emotional instability, sleep disturbances, eye-hand coordination problems, and sensitivity to stress. This is normal; there is no need for fear or shame. Stress management is one of the best antidotes for post acute withdrawal symptoms.

The task of recovery is to repair the damage done by addiction. It involves learning skills for a healthy life, and does not include the use of alcohol or other drugs. The potential for relapse is a normal part of recovery: it is unrealistic to believe that we will not experience problems or situations where the potential for relapse is strong. When these problems or situations are faced honestly, and with the appropriate support, they can be handled in positive ways. If allowed to fester, they will become a threat to recovery.

A successful recovery program requires a Twelve Step program and, for some individuals, the addition of professional counseling and therapy. Management of the long-term withdrawal symptoms is essential. We can't begin to tackle the larger issues of recovery if our bodies aren't cared for. Good nutrition is a must. Addiction to chemicals has damaged our bodies, and we need to repair them with a proper diet. Three balanced meals a day are important. If you need an in-between meal snack, choose healthy food: you're giving your body fuel to handle the stresses of recovery, so give it what it can really use. Because sweets, nicotine, and caffeine can stress the body, they should be avoided. Regular rest is also important. Lack of sleep and skimpy or skipped meals stress the body and make post acute withdrawal symptoms more likely. Treat yourself as if you're in training for the most important experience of your life. You are.

Post Acute Withdrawal

Research has shown that post acute withdrawal symptoms may contribute to relapse for many people.

Terence T. Gorski and Merlene Miller, in their book, *Staying Sober: A Guide For Relapse Prevention,* state, "Post acute withdrawal is bio-psycho-social syndrome. It results from the combination of damage to the nervous system caused by alcohol or drugs and the psycho-social stress of coping with life without drugs or alcohol."[2]

Stress is a major issue at this point simply because addicts are not familiar with managing their lives without chemicals; it's a new situation, and a frightening one. Stress triggers the brain dysfunction of post acute withdrawal and makes the symptoms worse. Therefore, the severity of the symptoms depends on how much stress the person is under in addition to the damage done to the brain by the addiction.

The symptoms are usually the worst between three and six months after sobriety begins, but the damage can be repaired with proper treatment. From a 6 to 24 month period, the symptoms usually get weaker if the recovery program is strong. Remember, it takes time for the symptoms to develop; thus, it takes time to heal.

Post Acute Withdrawal Symptoms

Each person will experience the following symptoms differently. Some people will be greatly affected by them, while others will not. In general, post acute withdrawal symptoms will get better over time and will become intermittent.[3] For some people, however, the symptoms will stay the same or worsen. These people are relapse prone.

1. *Inability to think clearly* (the brain periodically experiences mental lapses; concentration is short or impaired).
2. *Memory problems* (memories seem to disappear or return in scrambled form; this makes learning new skills and information difficult).
3. *Emotional overreactions or numbness* (overreactions are common, and you may feel as if you've used up all your emo-

tions and there's nothing left; moodiness may also become common).

4. *Sleep disturbances* (these are common, and include vivid or disturbing dreams that might make adequate rest difficult).
5. *Physical coordination problems* (may include dizziness, problems with eye-hand coordination, and slow reflexes; you may become accident prone).

Stress and Post Acute Withdrawal Symptoms

One of the biggest problems in recovery is judging what is a low-stress situation and what is a high-stress situation. During post acute withdrawal we are emotionally unstable and tend to overreact. Physically, we have been through an enormous change: we're abstinent. We're facing life in a new way. The presence of post acute withdrawal symptoms adds to the difficulty of coping. When the pressure of coping builds, the post acute withdrawal symptoms become worse. When things are going well, these symptoms may greatly diminish or even disappear.

If things aren't going well and the symptoms are strong, you may feel you're losing your mind. This isn't true — you are experiencing a normal part of recovery. If you become fearful or ashamed of these symptoms and isolate yourself, you will cause yourself more stress and put yourself in greater danger of relapse. Therefore, it's important that you begin to deal with the symptoms.

Does Anything Help?

First, you must take good care of yourself. As has already been mentioned, eat balanced meals and get enough rest. Also, exercise regularly. Pay attention to your recovery program — don't let it slide. The following are a number of other suggestions on how to handle post acute withdrawal symptoms:

1. Talk about what's happening to people who care about you and will understand. Other people following a Twelve Step program are good choices.

2. Don't minimize your situation; try to get everything out in the open.
3. Ask someone you trust if you're making sense. What you think is going on may be quite different from what is really happening.
4. Set goals and problem-solve with the situation at hand.
5. Think about the post acute withdrawal episode and see if you can discover a link between the onset of this episode and other episodes. Does a particular situation keep triggering the stress? If so, make plans to eliminate or curtail your involvement.[4]

It's important to learn what you can do for yourself. Post acute withdrawal puts your recovery in jeopardy, so learn what situations, people, and behaviors cause you the greatest stress. Once identified, stress can be interrupted or managed in such a way that you are not in danger.

Stuck Points

Because the process of recovery is not a straight line, with all tasks equally difficult, we can expect to experience some problems. We become stuck in recovery when we are faced with changes that seem beyond us. It may be as basic as learning to eat a balanced diet, or as complex as establishing an honest relationship. Whatever the task, it may appear larger than our ability to cope with it.

The positive thing to do at this point is to back off from the difficult situation for a while and approach it at another time. This lowers stress. Next, we can examine the situation rationally by discussing it with others. Then we can find the support we need to get through the stuck point successfully. When we're ready, we can make another attempt to complete the task.

Many recovering people react to difficulty with denial. By ignoring the problem, stress is increased. As the stress increases, post acute withdrawal symptoms occur or increase. This creates more problems, more stress, and more intense symptoms. In *Staying Sober,* Gorski and Miller point out, *"The person* becomes progressively more stressed. The increased stress leads to a state of free-floating anxiety and compulsion. The person feels compelled to do something, anything, to relieve the anxiety and compulsion, often adopting compulsive behaviors that temporarily relieve the stress. The compulsive behavior, however, produces additional long-term problems in exchange for the short-term relief. Eventually the stress leads to the activation of the relapse process and these people begin losing control."[5]

Another aspect of denial is that we may miss the warning signs of relapse until it's too late. When we deal superficially with the anxiety, other problems are created. In order to break the habit of denial we have to develop the habit of self-awareness.

What We Don't Know Can Hurt Us

When some people return to addiction, they feel that it is a positive option. In the recovery process, they might feel they have traveled a long road of despair and pain that has left them thinking they have few choices except insanity, suicide, or resumed use of alcohol or other drugs. Recovery has been an ordeal without rewards.

The rewards of recovery are great and can be experienced — this is demonstrated daily by people from all sections of society. What goes wrong in recovery starts with a series of mistaken beliefs about the disease of addiction and about the nature of recovery.

One of the most common mistaken ideas is that recovery means we are no longer using alcohol and other drugs, and that relapse is the resumption of use. We might think, when we're sober, we're recovered; when we're drinking or using, we're not. Black and white. This isn't true. Of course, as long as we're drinking or using, we are not in recovery, but recovery is much more than abstinence. Recovery is the rebuilding of our lives based on the principles of healthy living. It is a process, not a fact.

It is also quite common to believe that as long as we attend our A.A. or other Twelve Step support meetings, we're not at risk for relapse. We might think as long as we don't think about using or drinking everything is fine. If we've been in a Twelve Step program for any length of time, it's likely we've known people who were admirable in their attendance at meetings, but who relapsed anyway. It's important to attend meetings — that's where we get some valuable assistance — but the assistance is useful only if we're working and committed to the program. It's not realistic to think we'll never be tempted to use our drug of choice again; when the going is rough, we might fantasize about escape. This is normal, but the fantasies pass if we acknowledge them and get them out in the open.

Other areas of wrong thinking involve motivation and treatment. If we relapse, we tend to think that we're not motivated to recover, or that we need more pain in our lives to recover. This isn't true. Relapse occurs when the building blocks for recovery have not been used: we didn't stick with our Twelve Step program or get the appropriate counseling or both. We don't get just one chance at recovery unless the alternative is death. Likewise, it's a mistake to blame the treatment we received for our relapse. That puts all the responsibility on people who we think are supposed to heal us. That would truly be magic.

These mistaken beliefs can keep us stuck. The way to get rid of them is to become educated about the relapse process and become committed to working a Twelve Step program. With the proper knowledge, we can go on to make the necessary changes in both our thinking and our actions.[6]

Cross-Addiction

Once we stop drinking or using, we may want to replace the addiction with something "safe." If we start using another drug, this is called *cross-addiction*. It occurs most quickly when the new drug is similar to the original drug. For example, a person who has withdrawal symptoms after abstaining from prescribed sleeping pills might start using over-the-counter sedatives.

We can become addicted to other types of mood-altering drugs, though the dependency develops more slowly. If the second drug isn't as effective in deadening the pain as the first, we may crave the original drug. When under the influence of the new drug, we may mistakenly feel that returning to the original drug is possible.

This is not full recovery. Common second addictions to caffeine, nicotine, over-the-counter sleeping aids, diet pills, or marijuana occur when people believe that using these drugs is okay because they aren't using alcohol or "hard" drugs.

Research shows that alcoholics tend to consume a great deal of caffeine — more so than nonalcoholics. Caffeine is a stimulant and therefore alters our moods. When used heavily, caffeine can increase the risk of relapse because it increases irritability, anxiety, and the tendency to overreact.[7]

When you first stop drinking coffee or colas, you may notice withdrawal symptoms such as headaches, irritability, and emotional overreactions, but after a few days, these symptoms will pass.

Compulsive Behavior and Relapse

Another way of escaping reality in recovery is through compulsive behavior. These behaviors are healthy outlets for stress if done in moderation; however, when carried to extremes, they produce a similar short-term high as do addictive chemicals, followed by a similar return to pain. Some behaviors that can become compulsive are:

- eating or dieting;
- gambling;
- working or achieving;
- exercising;
- sex;
- thrill seeking;
- escape; or
- spending.

The behavior can become an addiction in itself. Gorski and Miller say, "Compulsive behaviors make you feel good in the short run but weaken you in the long run."[8] Sobriety means being free of compulsive behaviors as well as addictive chemicals.

Relapse and the Family

Family members can help or hinder one another in recovery. In *Staying Sober,* Gorski and Miller say, "Family members can be powerful allies in preventing relapse in the addict. . . . As family members become involved in relapse prevention planning, a strong focus is placed upon coaddiction and its role in family relapse. . . . Addiction is presented as a family disease that affects all family members, requiring them to get treatment."[9] Even if other family members aren't drinking or taking other drugs, they are affected by the behavior of the addict and, consequently, the family can become dysfunctional.

Stress is a primary problem for both the addict and family members. All of them are going through intense changes. When we live with other people, our changes affect them and their changes affect us. That's why it's important to protect each other from stress whenever possible. If the interaction between the addict and family members causes a great deal of stress, then appropriate counseling and intervention (a way of helping a person in crisis when he or she refuses to be helped) must be a part of the recovery program.

It's important to remember that everyone in the family is prone to dysfunction. Old behaviors are hard to eliminate for all of us. Addicts, for example, may be doing fine in their recovery programs, yet their families are losing control. Just as the addict makes plans to interrupt the relapse process, so must the family members.

The ideal in family relapse prevention is that everyone will work together. This, however, may not be possible. Therefore, it's important for us to work with those family members who are willing.

Alcoholics Anonymous' slogan, "One step at a time" is no idle cliche. In recovery, change takes time. Healthy change takes commitment, effort, and hope. To start again, to recover, means facing the truth about ourselves and learning to deal with our lives differently. There is always risk — the risk of relapse is present every day we are abstinent. But this risk is not a demon ready to undo our work in a moment of weakness. It is a situation we can use to aid us, to make us stronger.

CHAPTER 5

Needs and Choices

We have examined some developmental skills that influence our sense of self. Now, we will present another theory of growth, and examine the complex process of change. Numerous factors are involved when we decide to make a change, not all of them obvious. Even those factors we can't quickly identify influence us, sometimes more than we want. The more we're aware of these factors, the more we're able to work with them. This is another way that we can manage stress.

People who live the most satisfying lives are "self-actualized,"[1] according to Abraham Maslow, the behavioral scientist who coined the term. These are people who see life realistically. They don't make excuses for themselves but accept responsibility for their actions. Because they see themselves clearly, they can accept differences in others. They are creative, spontaneous, and highly motivated to develop themselves fully. They have met a series of basic needs — which we all share — and are able to concentrate on self-improvement.

People who are not self-actualized have not yet met these needs, either because they don't feel they can, because circumstances prevent them from doing so, or both. These people dwell on their deficiencies and tend to make decisions based on fear; they don't feel safe, loved, or valued.

Hierarchy of Needs

Maslow theorized a hierarchy of needs, with self-actualization at the top. We must satisfy each level before we are free to fully develop our talents. According to him, this is the highest achievement in life.

Of course, our physiological needs must be met first. These include our need for oxygen, food, water, and shelter. Because our society does a fairly good job of providing these needs, they are not generally strong in motivating a person to attain self-actualization. We also have a basic need for sexual expression. Next, we need to feel secure.

This involves maintaining personal safety and freedom from danger. We need a certain sense of order to feel safe. We need to feel that the police or our armed forces will protect us, or that we can in some way protect ourselves. If this need isn't met, we panic. The fight or flight syndrome commences, and we're unable to think of anything until this situation has been resolved.

Also, we have a need to belong and to be loved. We need to feel part of a family and community where we're wanted and able to share our goals and feelings with others. If we don't have this, we feel isolated, abandoned, and lonely. Because we live in such a technologically-oriented culture, many people struggle with this need. Our society is also highly mobile, and the small clans and communities that nurtured our parents and grandparents are no longer so prevalent.

Next, we all need recognition and esteem. We must feel that our efforts are worthwhile and appreciated by others. Praise, prestige, and success are very important.

Finally, we have a self-actualizing need. When we are self-actualizing, we are experiencing life fully. We understand ourselves and relate well to others. We're creative and confident. We have what Maslow calls "being-values." These include honesty, justice, and goodness. We're motivated to include beauty and play in our lives, and we strive to be healthy, positive, and good people. Self-actualizing people will stand up for what they believe even if it isn't popular.

Maslow also believes that self-actualizing people have peak experiences. These are moments filled with joy in which we see ourselves as united with the universe. These are times in which we feel whole, loved, and creative. These experiences can be realized in artistic or scientific efforts when everything seems to flow together. They can also occur during meditation or prayer, or at moments of profound emotional impact. Witnessing the birth of a child would qualify as a peak experience for most people. During these experiences, there is a transformation — a forgetting of self occurs. Our vision of reality can be altered, and we are suffused in joy.

Self-actualized people can be creative on two levels: with a specific talent or skill, and generally, as a way of approaching life. In their approach to life, they can be creative while cooking breakfast, playing weekend baseball, and washing their cars. In mundane as well as vital tasks, these people find alternatives and options for fulfillment.

If we each have the need to become self-actualized, why don't more of us do it? The major stumbling block to achieving this level is that we don't or can't meet our need for safety. This is a compelling need, and is often at odds with our equally compelling need to be self-actualized. Based on how we were raised, we may automatically choose what is safe and familiar, thereby negating our chances for a more fulfilling life. This reaction may not even be conscious. But it does exert great influence. Likewise, if we have learned to trust the world and have successfully formed our own identity, chances are we will choose to grow.

This habit of choosing growth is formed in exactly the same way as the habit of choosing safety — through many small experiences when we are encouraged to express our curiosity and creativity. It's possible to make positive choices every day that override the voice of safety, and to form a self-actualizing habit. Virtually everything we do, from taking a shower to making a speech to fixing a flat tire is an opportunity to become more fulfilled.

Then, over time, the choices we make to grow enhance our self-confidence and sense of control so that we feel safer than before. It's one of life's paradoxes that to feel secure, we need to test ourselves against the unfamiliar.

Another way of putting this is when we choose self-actualization, we are acting in our best interest. This involves listening to our inner voice, which may instruct us to act contrary to what we think will gain us the approval of others.

To listen to and know one's inner voice, Maslow makes the following suggestions:

1. Perceive more fully — how you feel and what you feel, what your senses tell you.
2. Choose to grow. When you are given the opportunity to experience life more fully, make a habit of choosing it.
3. Listen to your inner voice. In social situations, listen to what your inner voice is telling you rather than what others think is "right." (It may not be right for you!)
4. When in doubt, be honest. We can improve relationships by being honest. Others can't respond to us or give us what we need if they don't know what's going on with us.
5. Work to do the things you want to do well. Admit that your talents are worth developing, even though you may not be a genius.

Self-Awareness

Self-awareness is recognizing patterns in how we respond to what's going on around us. This is how we come to understand ourselves. It's how we know which needs are being met and which aren't. By taking a look at ourselves, we can identify the habits and automatic reactions we use to cope — positively and negatively. Self-awareness is a continuous process that involves a willingness to live in the present, and an acceptance of who we are. It becomes introspection when we evaluate and judge ourselves.

Turning off the internal critic is of prime importance in self-awareness, because it isn't the "oughts" and "shoulds" that lead to self-actualization. Most of us have far too good a relationship with our internal critic — to the point that every action is accompanied by the little voice that says we've done poorly. For self-awareness to become self-actualization, we are required to know our inner voice or guide, which is not critical of us. This voice is not our conscience, though it would seldom lead us to destructive behavior. It comes from the core of ourselves, is part intuition and part experience, part conscious understanding, and part unconscious desires. It lets us know what is best for us.

Developing rapport with this voice requires patience and concentration. For some of us, it also requires courage, especially if looking inward has not been a part of our lives.

The following exercise is designed to bring out the inner voice. If you are not familiar with this idea, practice the technique a few times. Once you develop a feeling for your inner voice, you will have established the foundation of self-awareness.

A Visualization Technique

1. Get into a comfortable position. Loosen restrictive clothing. Dim the lights. Eliminate as much external noise as possible.
2. Close your eyes. Take several slow, deep breaths. Gradually begin to focus on your body, starting at either head or toes. Ask yourself, How does it feel? If your head (or toes) are tense, breathe deeply and relax the muscles. Don't move on at this point until you feel relaxed. When you do, move on to other parts of your body. Continue until your whole body is relaxed.
3. Breathe deeply. Now, imagine yourself in a lovely grove of trees on a sunlit afternoon. In front of you is a shallow brook with stepping stones across it; on the other side is a giant oak in a flower-strewn meadow. This is where you want to go. As you cross the brook, take a deep breath. Going from stone to stone, breathe deeply and say to yourself, "I am becoming more relaxed. When I get to the other side, I will be completely relaxed." Do this at least ten times.
4. When you reach the other side, again tell yourself that you feel completely relaxed and peaceful. Imagine yourself walking toward the oak tree, and then settling comfortably beneath it. Rest here (but don't go to sleep) for a while. Allow whatever images that occur to you to pass without re-

action. If something disturbs you, bring yourself back to the oak tree in the meadow.

5. You are waiting for someone or something to arrive. It will be a comforting, friendly force; there is nothing critical or negative about it. Whatever shape it takes is appropriate (and it doesn't have to take the same shape each time). Animal, human, alien, mythical figure — whatever shows up is okay. You might feel like asking it questions: "What am I going to do about — ?" Or, you might just sit together, enjoying each other's company.

6. After a while, say good-bye in a friendly, affectionate way. Take a walk back over the brook. As you do so, say to yourself, "With each step I feel relaxed and rested. I am coming back now." When you are on the other side, count to three and open your eyes.

What did you learn? Does reading through the technique make you nervous? If so, why? By practicing this technique, you can get a stronger sense of who your inner voice is.

How We Change

We change whether we want to or not. Some of the greatest challenges in our lives come from unexpected sources — the crises and accidents that happen to all of us. But not all change is the result of surprise. We choose to make changes too. Some are more positive than others.

Part of the reluctance we may have about facing change is that we fear the unknown. For example, we may have the best intentions to stop smoking, but if the consequences are too indistinct or frightening for us, our attempts often fail.

We can, however, set ourselves up to succeed if we understand what is required of us to make the change. We'll refer to this as planned change; this is where new ideas and behaviors are created, tested, and adopted. Kurt Lewin, a psychologist who developed one theory of change, describes the process as having three steps:

unfreezing old behavior, moving to a new level of behavior, and then refreezing.[2]

Unfreezing is the phase of choice and motivation. Here we recognize the need for change. We look for information. What will it take for me to stop smoking? What are the benefits and drawbacks? This phase is complete when we understand that the change is in our best interests and will benefit us.

Then we move on to change our behavior. Here we have some sort of plan: "I'll quit cold turkey on Sunday," or "I'll cut down to two cigarettes a day."

We can structure our behavior because we've received information in one of two ways: through identification, or through scanning. In identification, we have seen the new behavior in someone we admire. Conversely, something awful — like lung cancer — may have happened to people we care about, and we identify with them enough to want to stop smoking.

In scanning, we get information from numerous sources. This reinforces our chances of success because from the beginning we are accepting more responsibility than through identification, where there is a tendency to focus on the source of inspiration.

A transition period follows when the new behavior becomes integrated into our personalities. This is known as refreezing. To refreeze, we need support and encouragement from others; this reinforcement is helpful because only some of the responsibility for support comes from within. We pat ourselves on the back as well as receive pats from others. Encouragement and positive feedback are necessary for new behavior to become fixed. That's why if you plan to stop smoking and everyone you know smokes, you should try to get support from those you might not ordinarily call on. This is where groups and organizations can help.

When we change, we should also be aware of the forces within us that both drive us to complete the change and restrict us in our attempts. Our need to become self-actualized is a motivating force. Our need to always maintain our security will restrain us.

How Big a Bite Are You Taking?

You can judge the difficulty of your plans by recognizing that there are simpler changes to make as well as harder ones.[3] The easiest kind of change to make is a change that doesn't affect our emotions; thus, we aren't likely to be challenged by it. We receive new bits of information daily: there is a storm moving in; traffic conditions on the freeway are fine; the price of milk is up. These bits of information could be very important to us if we predict the weather, control traffic flow, or run a dairy. But for most of us these are just new bits of information to fit into our lives.

The next level of difficulty involves changing our attitudes. This can be very difficult, and it requires substantial motivation because our emotions are involved. For example, before we enter recovery, we abuse alcohol or other drugs. Friends and loved ones may have expressed their concerns and tried to help us, but we denied there was a problem. Our attitudes formed this barrier of denial; our problems with chemical abuse and our behavior did not change until we faced the denial and admitted the unmanageability of our lives — the powerlessness we had over chemicals. Being honest and admitting the truth about ourselves — which is one of the most difficult things a person can do — led to a change in our attitudes, and caused us to commit ourselves to a recovery program.

An even more difficult task involves changing our behavior. This goes one step further than changing our attitudes. Acting on our beliefs is always more difficult than just having them because there are always consequences to actions. We may or may not feel ready to take responsibility for them.

Suppose you are ready to modify the way you feel and think about food, and join a group that supports weight loss. This time, it's more than a diet; most people would find this positive, but perhaps your spouse likes you the way you are. He or she is threatened by your actions. You are now in the position of defending your decision against your spouse — someone whose opinion matters to you. Are you going to drop out of the group and quit your diet to maintain peace at home? Are you going to challenge your spouse to change with you?

The most difficult changes to make are ones that must be agreed upon by a group of people. This is not surprising, considering that each person brings different motivations and restrictions to any change. But there are ways of succeeding. One important factor is how strong the communication network is among the participants. If all members feel comfortable about expressing their reservations as well as their enthusiasm, the change is likely to go through. In addition, each person must see the benefit of changing, and he or she must be clear about what will be accomplished. Even so, there can be unforeseen problems within the group.

The fact that groups are hard to change can actually be a blessing. Groups offer us stability that helps us meet our needs for safety. Because groups absorb change less readily than individuals, we can depend on them to reaffirm certain beliefs and behavior.

How Much Do You Really Want to Change Anyway?

All of us know from experience that not every attempt to change will succeed. If we manage to stop smoking, we might take it up again in two weeks. If we take up jogging for the summer, we may be relieved to give it up when the weather gets colder. Most of us have a list of changes we'd like to make, but many of them remain fantasies. We either lack the motivation to try or the motivation to stick to it. Why? It can be because we underestimate the power of our need to be safe.

The following list of questions is designed to reveal the depth of your willingness to change. Regardless of whether you want to color your hair or find a new job, you need to evaluate your feelings. Write out your answers if it will help clarify matters.

1. How important is this change to me?
2. How drastic a change am I thinking of?
3. How far does it differ from what I am doing now?
4. What will it require of me? Time? Money? Courage?
5. Who else will be involved? What do I expect of them?
6. Where will I get support and encouragement?
7. Where can I learn more about what it takes to make this change?
8. Who do I know who has gone through this change and will talk to me about it?
9. Is this the right time for me to make the change?

10. What stumbling blocks do I anticipate? How can I plan for them?
11. Do I feel secure enough to tackle this change?

You can see how important self-awareness is in this process. You can see, too, how valuable your inner voice is in motivating you toward growth. We've included some ideas to help you maintain your motivation, create a positive plan of action, and make a successful change.

1. Listen to your inner voice for a course of action in line with who you really are. Don't train for a marathon when you want to run five-mile races.
2. Choose a project you are really interested in or where you see a clear advantage. This will carry you through discouraging or frustrating periods.
3. Evaluate your circumstances realistically. Realize that if everyone around you watches TV every night, it may be hard for you to start reading books. Look for sources of encouragement and develop them.
4. Try out your new behavior under the best possible circumstances. It would be better to start your diet when you are not terribly stressed, or when you are not facing the holidays.
5. Understand that changes don't take place in a vacuum. Family members and friends will be affected by your new behavior. Discuss your plans with them, and enlist their support. They'll need to discuss their reactions with you, so plan to listen. Communication is important.
6. Don't try to fit a simple solution to a difficult problem. Acknowledge that some kinds of changes will require outside help. It is unreasonable to assume too that behavior is always the problem. For example, alcoholics do not solve all their problems when they stop drinking. Alcoholism is a complex disease and to deal with it requires the support of many people.

7. There will be some cost to you. Old habits and beliefs resist change. It will take time, effort, planning, and support to make a successful change.
8. Expect periods of doubt and frustration. This is inevitable. But doubt does not mean that the project lacks validity. This just means that the going is tough, and you'll need support to keep on with it. Voice your frustrations to a sympathetic friend or counselor — but choose one who will encourage you to continue.
9. Finally, forgive yourself for failed attempts. Despite our best plans, life sometimes intervenes to sabotage them. Take it easy. If the change is right for you, resolve to try again at a later time.

The Last Word

Self-actualization is a state brought about by small steps. Each time we act in our best interests, we get closer to it. The result of our efforts is self-acceptance, a greater sense of control over our lives, and a decrease in stress.

By knowing more about the change process, we are able to achieve successful experiences, or at least understand why our plans fail. Thus, change becomes something we can utilize rather than something we fear. We'll never be free from change, nor the stress that accompanies our efforts to adapt.

We can, however, develop the self-awareness to make choices that enhance our lives, even when the best choice is to wait and see.

CHAPTER 6

Support

We all need friends to keep ourselves balanced and healthy. Through our interactions with others, we learn more about ourselves — a process that continues throughout our lives. We learn how to give and take, how to make it through difficult times, how to celebrate. We learn the rules of living with one another, how to love, how to discipline and be disciplined. We learn about customs and traditions from our families and neighbors, and we, in turn, pass them on to our children.

Our support network, which may include family members, friends, co-workers, and various professionals such as doctors and clergy, provides the intimacy and advice that enable us to meet daily challenges. In crisis, they may give us material and emotional comfort. Or they may listen when we just want to gripe. They may be a constant and physical presence in our lives, such as with a spouse or parent; or we may connect with them once a year during the holidays.

A support relationship can be rich and varied, based on years of shared experiences, or limited to a special role defined by our professional lives. Whatever the context, these positive relationships have several things in common: trust, openness, understanding, respect, concern, approval, and in the deepest friendships, love. (At the end of this chapter are exercises helpful in evaluating your support relationships.)

Friends Keep Us Healthy

Most of us think of health as the absence of disease; that is, if we aren't suffering from symptoms, we are well. But, being healthy is much more than that. It is a state of physical, mental, and social well-being that we have a great deal of control over. We may not have much say over heredity or environment, but we do make choices regarding our eating, drinking, smoking, and exercising habits. We also make choices regarding the intensity and variety of social contacts. Just as it is possible to alter our negative eating or exercise habits, so it is possible to change the kind of relationships we have.

Increasing evidence supports the thesis that friends — we use this term to mean any positive, social relationship — play a vital role in keeping us healthy. Mortality studies show that single, divorced, or widowed people have a greater chance of developing virtually every major disease than married people of the same age. Their chances of dying from these diseases are also greater. Single people are more likely than married people to be hospitalized for depression, and they are more likely to commit suicide.

One study showed that pregnant women undergoing stressful events developed three times the number of complications if they had no close relationships than if they did.[1] Another study reported that among the general population, people with few friends had two to five times the mortality rate of those with close ties.[2]

A third study revealed that men laid off from their jobs adapted better if their social network was strong as opposed to those who were isolated.[3] In a fourth study, men from a close-knit Italian neighborhood in Pennsylvania were found to have a lower incidence of heart disease than the general population despite all other risk factors being the same.[4] (Interestingly, when this community began to have the same mobility and divorce rate as the rest of the country, the incidence of heart disease rose to the national average.) Still another study, this one concerning British women and depression, revealed that those without a close confidant were ten times as likely to be depressed as those with a close friend.[5]

When Do We Need Support Most?

We need our friends most in crises or during major transitions. It's often difficult for us to see exactly what's happening at these times, so our friends provide encouragement and clarity. They let us know that, yes, we can get through it, and yes, we will make the right choices. Sometimes they've experienced the same thing, and so can guide us.

The shock of losing someone close to us can cause a long period of disorientation. We may not be capable of completing even the simplest tasks, let alone making the difficult and frequently major decisions required of us. We are literally in need of assistance — from family, friends, neighbors, and advisors. This kind of devastating crisis is clearly a time to get all the support we can.

Sometimes a crisis affects a whole neighborhood or town, such as in the event of a flood, earthquake, or tornado. Although most communities have disaster relief programs, and organizations like the Red Cross provide assistance, it is often neighbors helping neighbors that make the biggest difference. When everyone is in trouble, everyone has a little something to share. This is a lesson people in rural communities know well: neighbors are important to our well-being and sometimes to our survival.

During the many transitions in our lives, friends are a factor in how well we manage. For example, youngsters anxious about entering high school will probably find solace in the company of other teenagers facing the same dilemma. Likewise, sympathetic, older students can answer questions, show them around, and reassure them that after the first few weeks, high school will be as familiar as junior high was. Teachers, counselors, and their parents, showing concern for their teenager's fears, will also make the transition easier for them. Since none of us can avoid this sort of transition, the stronger our social network, the more resources we can call upon to ease the way.

We can also use our social network when we see a hard time in the making. This could be a happy but intensely emotional event, such as the birth of a child. For a couple having their first baby, this period is full of questions, dreams, and fears. It may involve a major shift in livelihood as the mother or father stops working, perhaps for years.

The couple's relationship alters with the new responsibilities, and virtually every aspect of life is changed, including sleeping, eating, and sexual habits. The social structure may also change — old friends may or may not be able to relate to the new family — and there will be a need to form new relationships with people who will babysit and give counsel.

The young couple will need much support before the baby is born and during the early months of the child's life. By educating themselves about the process of becoming parents, they can line up both the personal and professional support they will need to meet the challenge. In this way, the couple can remove some of the stress involved. They will feel more relaxed because they have a strong support network to see them through any crisis. Also, they will feel more in control, and it is hoped, more able to enjoy their new child.

How Did This Happen Anyway?

Until about age three, we aren't much concerned with making or keeping friends. We're too concerned with learning to walk and talk and getting our basic needs met. Our focus begins to shift, however, when we recognize that there are other children in the world. Our first interactions are self-centered: we like another child's toy, and are attracted to the child who owns it. How else are we going to play with it? We can't tell the difference between our needs and other children's. If they need a glass of water, big deal. If we need a glass of water, it is a big deal! Our first friends are usually close to home. We like them for what they can do or what they've got or both.

From age four to nine we learn to differentiate between our needs and the needs of others. It's okay if our friend needs a drink of water, providing the time it takes to get it doesn't significantly interrupt our play. We like being with people who help us get what we want. Reciprocity is relatively unknown at this point.

We learn during our sixth to twelfth years that friendship is a two-way street. Good friends give as well as receive, although the goals still tend to be separate. For example, one child will be willing to get his or her friend a glass of water if afterwards they can both take a bike ride.

From about nine to fifteen, the friendship shifts to a mutually advantageous situation in which deep feelings are shared and conflicts resolved. The friendship involves mutual goals — something unknown before. The participants see the relationship as exclusive — even possessive. Best friends tend to be almost inseparable. If one of them wants a glass of water, the other may go along just to be there.

Young people from about the age of twelve have the ability to make more than one good friend. These friends may hang around together in cliques, their needs overlapping. Goals are generally the same, such as making it through school, and being popular. While very intense friendships still exist, both parties recognize and allow other friendships to develop.

Our ability to make friends evolves rapidly through adolescence. We rely on our friends to help us develop a sense of self as we grow up. They are often our safe haven. Friends also play an important role as we move away from home and start our own lives.

Once into our twenties we need a wider variety of friends than before; these friends relate to the many changes we experience.

Friends may be neglected when we marry and have children. Little energy is left over at this point to support numerous friendships. After a period of time, however, we need relief from these responsibilities, and we re-establish old connections or form new ones.

Throughout our lives, we retain the ability to make friends and to care for the ones we've already got. Old friends know where we've been; new friends know where we are. Both help us figure out where we're going.

What Do We Look for in a Friend?

We look for validation in our friendships. We seek a reflection of our own ideas and experiences, as well as those traits we admire and aspire to, such as loyalty, openness, a sense of humor, and warmth. We also might be drawn to people of the same age who share the same occupation, educational background, level of income, and religious, political, or social affiliations. These give us the common ground to begin and maintain a relationship.

RELAX, RECOVER

Oliver Wendell Holmes said, "There is no friend like an old friend who has shared our morning days, no greeting like his welcome, no homage like his praise." Our dearest friends, including the people we marry or live with, have our well-being at heart. Their concern and caring are important in our ability to meet life's challenges. In a mature and loving relationship, we are as blessed to give love as we are to receive it. When we are troubled or confused, we can speak to our friends of our heart's concerns plainly without fear of rejection, just as we can listen to them when they are in need.

We need friends with whom we can discuss issues of importance to us. A sympathetic world view or similar sense of humor could be important in this relationship. These friends tend to stay constant in our lives, and the relationship is characterized by numerous activities or experiences both parties enjoy.

We also might have a friend at work with whom we share mutual support — a relationship established formally by definition of our job as well as informally because we share rapport. We might share transportation to and from work with this person, or we ask him or her for a ride to work when our car is in the shop. In return, we are willing to provide the same service. Because we work with this person every day, there is a vested interest in maintaining the relationship. This is a powerful bond in itself, and many long-term friendships have been formed in this way. For the friendship to develop further, however, we would probably have to have more than just our jobs in common, especially if one or both parties leave the job.

Local gossip, the weather, politics — these are topics we discuss with any number of casual friends and neighbors. These friendships keep us involved with a larger world; we share information, validate our place in the community, and do favors for one another informally. Unless you live in a particularly stable community, the faces in this group may change quite frequently. Many neighborhood relationships never get beyond this, but there is a sense of trust and concern among the people involved.

Other Kinds of Friends
From the time we are small children, we band together in couples or groups of all boys or all girls. Culturally, we have a long tradition

66

of same-sex friends standing with us in good times and bad. With these friends we can relax and confide in one another.

Experiences unique to men and to women bond same-sex friends. Other activities are generally attributed to men or women, which the other sex typically doesn't enjoy. Shopping for clothes or hunting for deer typify these activities. These shared experiences yield some of our lives' most rewarding and enduring relationships. Our same-sex friends are dear to us by virtue of what we have in common. From childhood on, these friends probably will be a mainstay in our support network.

A rarer type of friendship is the one that develops between men and women, which excludes romance. These friendships are sometimes difficult to nurture unless both parties work at it. Difficult as these friendships may be to instigate, they are well worth the effort, for men and women have much to teach each other about meeting life's challenges.

Special Interest Groups

Groups formed to share information about a subject, or to create or promote various projects or interests, are also good places to make friends. Sewing circles, book clubs, sports clubs, political action groups, community service organizations, religious or social volunteer agencies, and travel groups are all formed so that people with similar interests can meet. In general, the smaller the group, the more intimacy is established among members. In larger groups, we may have to work harder to make the kind of contacts we want. But, in times of crises, these friendships can provide very valuable help. Some groups are organized specifically for that purpose.

Support Groups

Because of special needs, most of us at some point will join a group designed to help deal with a major and ongoing change. These groups are exemplified by Alcoholics Anonymous, whose primary purpose is to promote and support sobriety. Groups formed for such specific purposes are extremely helpful because each person in the group is experiencing the same problem; thus, the information and understanding available are meaningful.

These groups remove stress from people by giving them a framework for change — something families are often unable to do. Groups provide an arena to air grievances, anger, and fear in safety. They also provide an atmosphere of encouragement. These meetings are scheduled regularly, and people share their experiences with alcoholism in a supportive, nonjudgmental atmosphere. The meetings are structured to allow time for reflection, reaffirmation of the group's purpose and philosophy, and sharing. Anonymity is required; only first names are exchanged. After the meetings, members are encouraged to continue their rapport in informal gatherings.

The basis of A.A. philosophy rests in the Twelve Step recovery program. This program begins with a surrender of one's will and an acceptance of being chemically dependent, helping alcoholics to restructure their lives around positive principles. The regular meetings form the core of support within the alcoholic community, as people help each other work through the lifelong process of recovery.

New members choose sponsors, people they admire and trust. Sponsors agree to help the beginner with their program in whatever ways are appropriate. This usually means exchanging telephone numbers and being available at times of crisis or self-doubt. It also means helping with the development of a relapse prevention program as well as role playing or the practice of other new skills.

Numerous Twelve Step groups patterned after A.A. address addictions and compulsive behaviors, such as gambling and eating disorders. Family members of alcoholics or other drug addicts need to find their own groups to meet the challenge of their problems. These may include Al-Anon, Ala-tot, Alateen, and Adult Children of Alcoholics. These groups are based on the same Twelve Step program, with appropriate distinctions, and function similarly. If you plan to join such a program, remember to set yourself up for success at the very first meeting.

- Learn where and what time the meeting is held, and directions from your home.

- If possible, call ahead and arrange for someone to meet you there or to give you a ride.
- Arrive on time.
- Ask questions, if you feel you need to.
- Follow up and become involved. Talk to the members to learn who a good sponsor would be. Join others for coffee afterward.

Participation in some groups continues as long as you need it to; others have a graduation point when you are free to go it alone or to join a different support group for maintenance. Members often become very close to one another, like a second family.

Group Therapy

Group therapy has similar goals, but the members have a variety of problems instead of the same problem. Shyness, fear of success, anxiety about intimacy, difficulties with rejection or denial are some reasons people join group therapy. Through discussion with one another and counseling by psychiatrists, psychotherapists, or both, members gain insight into their behavior. Some problems, especially those of an intimate nature, are not usually brought up in group therapy, but almost everything else is. Here again the members form close bonds.

Participation in group therapy is determined by the facilitators involved. It lasts as long as both the therapist and the participants believe it should.

Groups, Groups, and More Groups

You always have the option of forming a group yourself. This can be a highly rewarding endeavor. Chances are, if you have a particular interest, others do too. Many neighborhoods have banded together to form Neighborhood Watch groups that look out for and report crime. The side effects of this effort can include better neighborhood relations, block parties, political lobbying on neighborhood issues, and car pools for school, sports activities, and work. Development of neighborhood projects such as bike paths, playgrounds, and summer activities can also be realized when the group expands to meet many common goals.

Are You a Good Friend?

Answering the following list of questions may give you some indication of how good a friend you are.

1. Do you keep your promises to do things?
2. Do you praise your friend's accomplishments or good fortune?
3. Can you restrain your competitive nature when necessary?
4. Do you support and encourage your friend when he or she is down rather than finding fault?
5. Do you enjoy seeing your friend succeed?
6. When you do a special favor for a friend, can you keep quiet about it?
7. Can you keep a secret when trusted with one?
8. Do you return favors?
9. Would you be there if your friend needed help?
10. Are you interested in your friend's life outside of your relationship?
11. Can you allow your friend to be in a bad mood?
12. Can you forgive your friend for not living up to your expectation?
13. Do you know when to go home?

If the answer was yes to most of these questions, you're a good friend to have. If the answer was no to most, remember that no one is perfect. Improvement is in order. This may be a good time to call on your friends for support.

What Makes a Friendship Work?

All friendships experience fluctuations. At times they are satisfying and rewarding with little effort. At other times it is necessary to straighten out misunderstandings or problems that may require much effort. Because each of us is constantly changing, our relationships change too.

Several communication skills are involved in making a friendship work, and they depend on a positive sense of oneself. Simply put, you value yourself and thus your friend. You are probably already familiar with some of these skills.

1. Each of you is separate from the other. You share thoughts and experiences without losing your identity.
2. Each of you values your time together, but can exist apart.
3. Each of you feels free to discuss anything relevant to the friendship.
4. Each of you is responsible for your own happiness; you don't blame your friend for your unhappiness.
5. Each of you will work at making the relationship better.
6. Each of you acknowledges that the other is growing, and you support these changes.
7. Each of you realizes that having fun is an important part of your friendship.
8. Each of you responds to the other in time of need.
9. Each of you has other meaningful relationships.
10. Each of you is committed to the other.

You can do numerous things to prepare yourself for stronger friendships. Positive attitude changes help promote free and sympathetic interactions. They enable you to recognize potential friends and potential close friends.

1. Be tolerant of the other person.
2. Recognize conflicts as they arise; solve them positively.
3. Express your feelings to the other person about how your relationship is affecting you; listen to the other person's feelings as well.
4. If you fear rejection, acknowledge it; stay in the relationship anyway.

5. Instead of assuming the feelings and opinions of others, learn what they really are.
6. Take risks and open up in order to receive the benefits of intimacy.
7. Stay curious about both your own emotions in the relationship and your friend's. Expect change.
8. Refrain from trying to meet the expectations of either yourself or your friend. You are not perfect, and it would be difficult to love you if you were.

In every relationship there will be hard times. Periods of doubt, anger, boredom, and frustration will occur. The clearer you are with your feelings, the easier it will be to get to the bottom of whatever problems caused these lapses. With both of you committed to the friendship, solutions are possible.

Barriers to Friendship
Many of us make assumptions about ourselves and other people that block the development of friendships. Obviously, thinking of people as stereotypes will harm positive interaction. To some extent, we are all guilty of this. We might group together by race, religion, or nationality those people whose differences seem threatening. We don't need to participate in stereotyped thinking; it does nothing for us. On the contrary, it cuts us off from people who may greatly enrich us.

Another barrier is shyness. While we have probably all felt shy at some point in our lives, some people are so severely affected that they become socially isolated. Shyness often stems from low self-esteem and fear of rejection. It is also rooted in the need to meet impossibly high expectations that have little basis in reality. Exposing our imperfect selves to others can be frightening. We try to avoid it. Thus, this attitude makes developing intimacy with someone else extremely difficult. When we recognize that each of us is flawed, shyness begins to recede. Others seldom judge us as harshly as we judge ourselves.

SUPPORT

A third common barrier to friendship is the fear of being rejected. This is usually based on past experience. Most of us have had some painful encounters with people we really cared for — dates were refused, offers of friendship ignored, and relationships turned sour because the other person lost interest. We are likely to remember the pain long after we've forgotten whatever joy and happiness existed. These memories may keep us from reaching out to new friends because we fear a repetition of the past. While this may seem a normal way to cope for a short time, it is against our self-interest in the long run. There is no way to predict the future. To remain so self-protective only hurts ourselves. If we can look objectively at the past and learn from our mistakes, we are not likely to repeat them.

Most of us feel the constraints of time. We juggle many roles in our lives, and often the time needed to relax and renew ourselves in the company of friends is squeezed out. Because much more effort is involved in making new friends as we grow older, we tend to ignore this area entirely. Old friends can certainly help us cope with change. But new friends can offer us fresh ideas and insights into who we are.

Look also at what you have to offer. Your ability to be a good friend needs to be flexed as much as your muscles and your mind.

Ways to Beat the Barriers

Here are eight ways to overcome obstacles to solid friendship.

1. If you have a tight schedule, schedule time off with your friends each week.
2. If you are unable to see your friends frequently, call or write notes to them.
3. Establish personal traditions or rituals — for example, Friday night movies followed by coffee, semiannual fishing trips, or volunteer projects.
4. Give small gifts of appreciation; take each other to lunch or dinner.
5. Ask if you can do anything for them. Follow through if the answer is yes.
6. Ask for help if you need it.

7. Take a class together. Learning new skills with a friend will reinforce your chances of success.
8. Hug your friends. Hugs are nonverbal expressions of affection, concern, acceptance, vulnerability, joy, and love.

Plants and Animals Are Also Friends

A study of nursing home residents revealed that mortality decreased among those who were asked to care for a plant.[6] They were instructed to not only water it and make sure it got enough light, but to speak to it. The survival of both the plants and the elderly clients improved. This study brings out an important point: we thrive in relation to other living things.

Likewise, caring for a pet can be a vital part of our well-being. Most of us have known the pleasures of owning a pet. Here is a creature who seems to appreciate us no matter what. We don't have to explain our actions or moods to a dog or cat, and, in return we take care of them. Pets can prove powerful buffers against loneliness, depression, and apathy. If you doubt that they can be good friends, look at the grief some people suffer when their pets die. The attachment is profound.

We have a deep-seated need to care for living entities, and if you have been cut off from this experience, consider a house plant, goldfish, or, where appropriate, a puppy or kitten.

Balancing the Network

We will face stressful challenges, and these challenges will require utilizing our resources for resolving the stress. As a bulwark against those times, we need to maintain a healthy network of support, and to balance our efforts to make sure we don't overdo ourselves. Because we live in such a mobile society, it's important to spend at least some time each month reaching out to our friends. We'll never outgrow the need for friends, and, as we mature and the nature of our needs change, we need to have the fresh insights that new relationships bring us.

Likewise, it's important to spend time assessing long-term relationships to determine if they still work for us. If not, how can we improve them? It's a rare delight when we can sit with someone we haven't seen in years and seem to pick up where we left off. Most friendships, however, aren't like that: they need fairly constant care to function properly.

It isn't a mistake to limit the kind of relationships we choose to have, so long as we recognize that, in crises, we will need a variety of friends to help us make it through. The key is how satisfying these relationships are. Do we feel comfortable and nourished by them? Are we able to comfort and nourish our friends? Asking and giving help are two sides of the same coin, and the foundation of any loving friendship.

What follows is a questionnaire to help you clarify your support network.

MY SUPPORT NETWORK

I. Fill out the following section, listing one or more persons.
    1. Spouse or significant other: _____
    2. Parent(s), if living: _____
    3. Brother(s), sister(s): _____
    4. Other relative: _____
    5. Female friend: _____
    6. Male friend: _____
    7. Co-worker: _____
    8. Clergy member: _____
    9. Counselor: _____
    10. Neighbor: _____
    11. Other supportive person: _____

II. If the following events happened to you, which of the above people would you call on for material or emotional support?
    1. If you felt shaken after a noninjury car accident? _____
    2. If you were diagnosed as having a serious illness? _____
    3. If your pet was run over? _____
    4. If you had an argument and felt angry? _____
    5. If you felt alone, depressed, or bored after a bad day? _____

6. If you got a promotion at work? _____
7. If you were having financial problems? _____
8. If you failed a course in school? _____
9. If you completed your first ten kilometer race? _____
10. If you won the state lottery? _____
11. If today were the anniversary of the death of someone close to you, or the anniversary of your divorce? _____
12. If your house were destroyed by flood or fire? _____
13. If today were your birthday? _____

III. How many individuals listed in Section I were listed in Section II?
   If you listed:
       0 - 2 persons = You are probably depending on too few friends; your network is very weak. Consider taking steps to expand it.
       3 - 5 persons = Your circle of friends will support you in most stressful situations, but it is still too weak to provide you with the balanced support you need in a crisis.
     6 or more persons = You are well-supported. Your network is broadly based, and will see you through even the most difficult times.

STRESS AND FRIENDSHIP

The following exercises will illustrate the relationship between support systems and your stress level.

First complete the stress level and network strength sections below:

Stress Level

Circle each stress event you experienced within the last twelve months. Then add the scores for each item you circled and put the total next to *Stress Total* on the next page.

Personal
(6) Serious injury or illness
(6) Alcohol, other drug, or emotional problem
(4) Marriage

(4) Death of close friend
(2) Trouble with friends or neighbors
(2) Begin or end school or training program

Work & Finances
(6) Lost job, retired
(4) Sold or bought home
(2) Changed jobs, promotion
(2) Trouble with boss

Family
(10) Death of spouse or immediate family member
(8) Divorce
(6) Reconciliation or separation
(4) Serious illness or injury of family member
(4) Pregnancy or birth
(4) Family arguments or trouble with in-laws
(4) Child enters or leaves home
(2) Relative moves into household
(2) Moved to new residence

Stress Total:

Support Network Strength
Circle one response for each item. Then add the scores and put the total next to the *Stress Total* on the next page.

1. At work, how many persons do you talk to about a job hassle? none (0); one (1); two or three (2); four or more (3)
2. How many neighbors do you trade favors with (loan tools or household items, share rides, babysitting, etc.)? none (0); one (1); two or three (2); four or more (3)
3. Do you have a spouse or partner? no (0); several different partners (2); one steady partner (3)
4. How often do friends and close family members visit you at home? rarely (0); about once a month (1); several times a month (4); once a week or more (8)

5. How many friends or family members do you talk to about personal matters? none (0); one or two (6); three to five (8); six or more (10)
6. How often do you participate in a social, community, or sports group? rarely (0); about once a month (1); several times a month (2); once a week or more (4)

Support Total:

If your Stress Level score is:
Less than 10: You have a low stress level and your life has been stable in most areas.
10 - 15: You have a moderate stress level and there has been a lot of change in your life.
16 or more: You have a high stress level and there have been major adjustments in your life.

If your Support Network score is:
Less than 15: Your support network has low strength and probably does not provide much support. You need to consider making more social contacts.
15 - 19: Your support network has moderate strength and likely provides enough support except during periods of high stress.
20 or more: Your support network has high strength and it will likely maintain your well-being even during periods of high stress.

CHAPTER 7

Exercise

Why Exercise?

People exercise for a variety of reasons: to build self-esteem, socialize, keep in shape, feel better, and to keep their stress level under control. The importance of exercise in stress management cannot be overemphasized. Regular exercise provides many tools for dealing with the demands of daily life.

When you exercise, you are working not only your muscles — where much tension is harbored — but your heart and lungs. You burn calories, tone muscles, and release pent-up energy. If overeating is a problem, exercise will help control your appetite. You feel a sense of well-being with exercise that carries over into other aspects of life. Most of all, exercise is a habit that enhances your life rather than erodes it.

Developing an exercise program can be a rewarding and satisfying experience. You can create a program unique to your interests and abilities that fits into your schedule and that satisfies a variety of needs.

Did you enjoy running races as a child? Riding your bike after school? Taking dance classes? Swimming at the neighborhood pool? These activities can easily become part of an adult fitness program. If you enjoyed physical exercise because you were with friends, find exercise classes or groups that will satisfy your need to socialize and to receive the support you need to keep going. Or, if you enjoy being on your own, you might relish exercise time to sort out your day.

In this chapter, we'll begin with an overview of types and benefits of exercise. Then we'll prepare you for self-assessment that will aid in choosing activities. If you have questions or doubts along the way, please contact your physician. Remember, the better you prepare, the more successful your program will be.

Types of Exercise

There are three basic types of exercise designed to increase flexibility, strength, and endurance. Flexibility exercises stretch the muscles and prepare the body for more rigorous activity. These exercises are a part of any exercise program in order to prevent injury. Stretching should be done at the beginning and again at the end of an exercise session. The type of stretching differs with the activity. For example, a dancer might focus on stretching the inner thighs, calves, and rib cage to prepare for kicks and bends, while a runner might pay special attention to the calves and thighs to prevent cramps.

Weight lifting or waterskiing are common types of static, isometric, or strength-building exercise. This type of exercise plays one force against another, causing muscles to swell. This helps muscles work more efficiently, but the benefit is limited to the muscle group you're working on.

For example, to build up the muscles in your upper arms, use dumbbells three or four times per week in a repetitive sequence. If you do nothing else, only your upper arms will benefit. A successful weight-training program focuses on many muscle groups. The benefit of weight training, also called *anaerobic exercise,* is muscle development, an increase in lactic acid tolerance so that you have less pain as you do more muscle building. At most gyms you can find weight training equipment and people who know how to use it properly.

The third type, endurance exercise, is also known as *aerobic exercise.* Aerobics promote cardiovascular fitness by requiring the lungs and heart to use oxygen more efficiently. Any rhythmical activity that moves large muscle groups for a prolonged period is considered aerobic. Swimming, cycling, walking, and running are all endurance exercises.

A well-rounded exercise program would include segments devoted to each kind of exercise, but we want to emphasize endurance activity because of its role in stress management. The changes that take place in our bodies during and after aerobic exercise are extremely important in combating the effects of stress. A lower heart rate and increased lung capacity are two critical physical advantages, while an increased sense of well-being is an emotional advantage. Aerobic exercise will increase strength and muscle tone, and all the body's major systems will benefit.

Emotional Benefits of Exercise

Since stress affects every area of our lives, exercise can be an important tool for rebalancing ourselves. Too often pressure to change our way of life becomes merely a series of negative, morale-slumping statements: Quit smoking! Lose weight! Eat better! Exercise, however, is positive. It can help fill the void left by our old ways of dealing with stress, which may have included drinking, overeating, or smoking.

You can create a new exercise habit. By giving yourself an area for growth and by setting goals (walking two miles in half an hour or completing a five-mile run), you learn to deal with stress in a healthy way. The increased sense of well-being will become as important to you as that drink or those chocolate chip cookies once were. Moreover, success in this area will give you confidence to tackle more difficult areas of your life.

You may feel that exercise is boring, repetitive, and purposeless at first. You might resent the time taken away from sleeping or watching television. You might feel foolish, or begin to compare yourself to the guy down the street who runs marathons. Give yourself the chance for exercise to become part of your life. Persistence will yield positive results.

Initially, you may notice a change in your mood: regular exercise provides a gentle lift. Then, as your program becomes more established, you'll find that you're uneasy when you skip a session. You just don't feel right. Your body grows accustomed to the effort.

These factors are important in setting up a successful exercise program:

- Begin at an appropriate level.
- Get a friend or family member to work out with you.
- Set a regular time for your sessions: three times a week for at least twenty minutes.
- Choose activities you enjoy.
- Maintain a positive attitude: decide to do it, then do it!
- If it helps, keep records of your sessions.

Physical Benefits of Exercise

The increased sense of well-being that comes with regular exercise is a complex biological process. It involves the cardiovascular, respiratory, endocrine, and muscular-skeletal systems. Exercised muscles are able to take more oxygen from the blood by increasing the capillary blood vessels supplying each muscle fiber. As a result, your body benefits from improved oxygen delivery. Metabolic capacity is also increased. Carbohydrates in the form of glycogen are increased, and lactic acid production is decreased.

In the cardiovascular and respiratory systems, aerobic exercise results in increased cardiorespiratory capacity and endurance; the lungs can utilize greater amounts of oxygen while the heart processes blood more efficiently. Thus, you have greater endurance as well as strength. Heart rate and blood pressure are reduced. Your resting heart rate will decline. A decrease from 85 beats per minute to 60 or less would save 1,500 beats per hour and more than a million beats per month. With every beat, stroke volume is increased and cardiac irritability and blood coagulability are decreased. Both are factors in heart attacks.

Aerobic exercise plays an important role in maintaining the proper weight, body composition (the relationship of fat and muscle), and appetite[1]. Exercise burns calories and promotes fat breakdown. Hormones released during exercise free up fat, which can be used for energy production. This increase in the circulation of free fatty acids may continue for hours following exercise.

Does It Really Work?

The following are some of the psychosocial benefits of aerobic exercise:

1. Exercise can produce a feeling of well-being.
2. Exercise has a tranquilizing and muscle-relaxing effect.
3. For some people, exercise is useful in reducing mental depression.
4. Exercise helps produce sound sleep.
5. Exercise increases stamina as well as resistance to fatigue.
6. Exercise can result in improved appearance through reducing body fat and improving muscle tone.
7. Exercise might improve self-control and self-confidence, producing a positive body image. Increased sexual performance may result.
8. Exercise provides motivation for improving health habits, including cessation of smoking and moderation in food and alcohol consumption.
9. Exercise may provide a means of fellowship with family and friends.
10. For many people, exercise increases job satisfaction and productivity; lower absenteeism has been reported among workers in exercise programs.
11. Exercise can inhibit the decline of many physical capabilities associated with aging. These include loss of strength, vigor, flexibility, and youthful appearance. Ongoing regular activity may postpone the thinning of bones that is of special concern for post-menopausal women.[2] Clinical investigation confirms that elderly people who exercise are fitter than young people who don't.

Convinced? The evidence is hard to ignore. What's your next step?

Pre-Exercise Assessment

Before starting a program, you need to determine just where you stand. The first question to ask is simple: How old are you? If you are under age 35 and free of medical complications, you should be able to begin an exercise program without in-depth testing. If you are over 35 or suffering from medical problems, you and your physician need to confer.

The next question is: Are you male or female? Since men contract coronary heart disease earlier and in greater numbers than premenopausal women, men might want to consult with their physicians.

The third question is: Has there been coronary heart disease in your family? Did either parent die or have heart problems before age 60? If so, a visit to the doctor is in order.

The next set of questions involve things we can change:

- Do you smoke?
- Are you overweight?
- Do you have high blood pressure?
- Do you lead a sedentary life?
- Do you have elevated cholesterol and triglycerides?

The answers to these questions will help build a complete picture for you and your physician of your present state of health.

The next step is to learn what your endurance level is. For those under 35 and in good health, we recommend Dr. Brian Sharkey's Physical Activity Index. The Physical Activity Index shows you how to evaluate your current fitness level based on the intensity, duration, and frequency of exercise.

PHYSICAL ACTIVITY INDEX

Calculate your activity index by multiplying your score for each category. Your score equals *intensity* times *duration* times *frequency*. Let's say your activity level of exercise is moderately heavy; thus, your score in the *intensity* category is 3. You exercise 45 minutes per session; your *duration* score is 4. You exercise 3 times a week; your frequency score is 4. Your combined score (3 X 4 X 4) is 48, which on the Evaluation and Fitness Category scale means your level of exercise is fair, but could be improved.

	Score	Activity
Intensity	5	Sustained heavy breathing and perspiration
	4	Intermittent heavy breathing and perspiration — as in tennis, racquetball

84

	Score	Activity
	3	Moderately heavy — as in recreational sports and cycling
	2	Moderate — as in volleyball, softball
	1	Light — as in fishing, walking
Duration	4	Over 30 minutes
	3	20 to 30 minutes
	2	10 to 20 minutes
	1	Under 10 minutes
Frequency	5	Daily or almost daily
	4	3 to 5 times a week
	3	1 to 2 times a week
	2	Few times a month
	1	Less than once a month

Evaluation and Fitness Category

Score	Evaluation	Fitness Category
100	Very active lifestyle	High
60 to 80	Active and healthy	Very good
40 to 60	Acceptable (could be better)	Fair
20 to 40	Not good enough	Poor
Under 20	Sedentary	Very poor

Source: Dr. Brian Sharkey. *Physiology of Fitness.* Champaign, Ill.: Human Kinetics Publishers, Inc., 1984.
Index score is highly related to aerobic fitness.

If you are over 35 or suffering from a medical problem, then we recommend a stress test that is arranged through your physician. This test involves pedaling a stationary bicycle or walking on a motorized treadmill while your heartbeat, electrocardiogram, and blood pressure are monitored. (It's also possible to have your oxygen consumption monitored as well.) In one to three minute increments, the level of exercise is increased until you have reached your maximum level of exertion. This test checks your fitness level, plus it will detect cardiac problems that could become serious if you start a strenuous exercise program. With these results, you and your doctor can plan a safe exercise program.

METs

During your testing, or throughout your fact-finding tour of exercise, you may run into the term "MET." A MET is a unit used to measure and compare how much oxygen a person uses during exercise with how much oxygen is used when at rest.

For example, if you are lying down, you're using one MET. As you increase activity, you gradually use more oxygen: sitting takes more oxygen than lying down, and a brisk jog takes more oxygen than walking slowly around the park. If you are walking at a three-mile per hour rate, you are using approximately 3.3 METs.

The better shape you are in, the higher the MET level you can tolerate. On a treadmill, for example, your MET level, or the amount of work you do, will be measured. In designing your program, it is important to start slowly — at a low MET level — because your ability to use oxygen must be given a chance to grow at a reasonable pace.

Once you've got a clear picture of your capabilities, there are some basic facts about exercise you should know:

Intensity. How hard you work out will determine how much energy you use.

Duration. How long you work out will determine how much energy you use.

Frequency. Exercising three times a week will maintain conditioning.

Muscle mass. The larger the muscle mass that's exercised, the more energy you will use. Thus, leg exercise uses more energy than arm exercise.

Economy of muscle activity. The better shape you're in, the less energy you will use. The more skill you have at running, for example, the more efficient your muscles become at running. In the beginning, you'll use more energy because the muscle groups aren't developed yet. So it is imperative to start walking or running on level ground in order to progress to running in the hills.

Environmental conditions. Heat, cold, and smog affect how difficult it is to exercise. With smog, refrain from exercising in a First Stage Alert. It is more hazardous to do so than to skip the exercise session. But if it is smoggy, yet not the extent of an alert, it is better to exercise than not. It is always best to design an exercise program that takes advantage of both indoor and outdoor exercise so that you can switch with fluctuations in weather and air quality.

What Does Aerobic Exercise Take?

An aerobic exercise program typically consists of three 20 to 30 minute exercise sessions per week. After stretching and warming up at a low level, you work out 20 to 30 minutes at 70 to 85 percent of your maximum heart rate. This rate is your target training range. One equation used in calculating the target training range is 220 minus your age (this number is your maximum predicted heart rate) multiplied by .75, which equals your target heart rate. By subtracting ten from your target heart rate you have your target training range. The Target Training Ranges chart lists target ranges appropriate for various ages.

TARGET TRAINING RANGES*

Age	Target (75% of Max.)	Maximum heart rate
20	140-150	200
25	136-146	195
30	133-143	190
35	129-139	185
40	125-135	180
45	121-131	175
50	118-128	170
55	114-124	165
60	110-120	160

Age	Target (75% of Max.)	Maximum heart rate
65	106-116	155
70	103-113	150
75	99-109	145

*220 − age ($\times$ .75) − 10 = target training range

You will benefit from the exercise if you work at 65 percent of your maximum predicted heart rate, especially if you increase the time you exercise. If you have been inactive for a long time, this level would be better for safe exercise.

For example, if you are unable to jog two miles in twenty minutes, you will benefit equally by walking three miles in 45 minutes. Conversely, jumping rope is much more strenuous than walking or jogging, so you wouldn't need to jump rope for as long as you jog. At the end of your session, a cool-down and stretching period allows the body to return to rest gradually. This cycle is designed to ease your body into strenuous activity and then out of it again without injury or major discomfort.

Tolerating Exercise

How well you tolerate exercise will depend on whether the intensity of exercise is appropriate for your level of fitness. Obviously, you won't start out a jogging program by running seven minute miles if you haven't run a quarter mile since childhood. Check how well-suited your program is by using the following guidelines.

Evaluate your respiration. You should always be able to say a full sentence on one breath of air. If you can't, you're doing too much. Think about going up a flight of stairs. Most of us have taken stairs too fast, and lost our ability to converse in the process. We're pushing too hard.

Check your pulse. Do this before, during, and after exercise. You can find your pulse by placing one or two fingers on the thumb side of the opposite hand just below the bone in your wrist. Another convenient place is below the jaw on either side of the thorax (Adam's apple) — press lightly when checking your pulse here; you don't want to stop circulation to your head and pass out. Your resting pulse rate, taken before you begin your session, is important because it changes with the intake of caffeine or alcohol, with smoking, lack of sleep, or increased stress.

Count your heartbeats for ten seconds, then multiply that number by six to find your pulse for a minute. The following is a brief list of conversions:

If your ten second rate was:	Then your minute rate is:
11	66
13	78
15	90
17	102
19	114
21	126
23	138
25	150

A pulse rate that stays too high following exercise — way above 100 or where it was at the peak of exercise — indicates that you've pushed too hard. Eventually you will instinctively know what your pulse is and where it should be, both at rest and during exercise.

If you feel you are working to 75 percent of your capacity even though your heart rate is low, there is no need to work any harder. Your muscles may be working as hard as they can. You may need to rest at intervals, especially in the beginning, because your muscles aren't used to the activity. It's still important to check your pulse, but also consider how your muscles feel.

If you go home after exercise and feel like taking a nap, or if you suffer insomnia at night and haven't had that problem before, you have probably been overexercising. Some days you just won't be able to get your body moving. That's normal. Your body is asking for rest, so either cut back or skip the session.

Not all of us are able to evaluate our blood pressure on the spot. But for those who have access to a blood pressure machine, the difference between the diastolic (bottom number) and systolic (top number) pressures should increase with exercise. (Generally, the diastolic stays the same while the systolic rises.)

The Ball Is in Your Court

If you are in a recovery program, you may need help determining realistic exercise goals. You may have a difficult time setting limits for yourself. Since exercise is a lifelong project, you need to formulate goals that will prevent injuries.

With the information presented here, you can go on to investigate a particular activity or group of activities that appeal to you. Warm-up and cool-down exercises differ from sport to sport, so make sure you consider this when you put together your routine. At first you may not be able to work out as hard or as long as you did in your adolescence. Remember, though, that gradual improvement will enable you to achieve a level of conditioning that will greatly enhance your life and decrease your stress level.

CHAPTER 8

Meditation

Learning to relax and let go is central to stress management. Many techniques are available to help us do that. These techniques are drawn increasingly from ancient philosophies, as well as modern research. They all have the same goal in mind: focusing attention.

Sound simple? It is, and it isn't. The techniques all require a quiet place relatively free from distraction, comfortable clothes, a relaxing position, and a passive attitude. Although these factors may require you making some adjustment, they are not too difficult to achieve.

With the exception of biofeedback, the techniques require only those props that free us from interference and enhance our ability to concentrate. Take the phone off the hook, and dim the lights. Cutting yourself off from the immediate stressors in your environment will set the stage for turning inward. Then, in whatever position is appropriate for the technique you've chosen, simply begin.

Now you have come to the hard part. At first, you will find that emptying your mind is a difficult task; it wants to continue racing through the concerns of your life at top speed. After all, you have a lot to do! Whether the technique you choose requires you to open up to or close down stimuli, ask yourself to stop judging, organizing, and worrying. Let it happen. Let yourself exist wholly in the present. Rest and yet be completely aware.

Choosing the right technique will depend on two things: what you want to accomplish, and what feels comfortable to you. Some techniques can be practiced many times during the day without removing you from your normal routine. Simply remembering to breathe deeply from time to time will break the stress response. Other, more complex techniques will require one to three sessions a day, usually lasting from fifteen to twenty minutes. You may focus on relaxing muscles, heart rate, or blood pressure. Still other techniques involve healing images that can take you away from daily cares via visual or auditory cues. Several techniques can be used to modify behavior, such as losing weight or stopping smoking.

This chapter will include instructions on breathing, progressive relaxation, and meditation. Chapter Nine will cover a wide range of alternative techniques that can be used alone or combined with other programs. Biofeedback will also be discussed in Chapter Nine. All of these techniques require patience and practice. As with exercise, you are building a habit, and habits take time to develop.

As you read through these chapters, ask yourself the following questions:

- Is this technique appropriate for me?
- Does it accomplish what I want it to?
- Can I integrate it into my schedule?
- Am I willing to commit to the sessions?

Many people eventually use several techniques, depending on what they want to achieve. But the basic steps of deep breathing and muscle relaxation form the foundation of nearly every program. Although you may know when you are tense, you may have to learn what it feels like to be relaxed. Being relaxed does not mean that you turn into a zombie. Quite the opposite. When you clear a path through the mind, you think more clearly. You can look at the practice of meditation as a way of prioritizing, a time out to refocus your thoughts. Where your mind focuses, your body will follow.

The first lesson will be in the deep breathing that is the foundation of all relaxation techniques. When stressed, we breathe shallowly. Often we simply maintain this rapid, shallow breathing pattern, sometimes speeding up or slowing down a little. But seldom do we take that long, deep breath which cues our body that the fight or flight response is complete.

A Breathing Exercise

Instead of filling the upper lungs with air, start by filling the lower lungs. Your stomach will expand, then your chest. This is how you breathed as a child. Slowly exhale, releasing all the air you can. Repeat. Now inhale and hold your breath for a few seconds, then release. Repeat. Slow down your breathing as much as you can. At first you may feel like you're hyperventilating, but you're not. Pay attention to how you feel as the air flows in, as you pause, and as you release the air. Are there any changes in your body? Imagine drinking in good air, and releasing bad. Your body will benefit from the increase in oxygen supply. You have given your body the signal that the fight or flight syndrome is over. Now your body can return to balance.

Practice deep breathing frequently, especially when you are stressed. If you wake up tense, take a few moments to breathe deeply before rising. Throughout the day, when you become annoyed or impatient, breathe deeply again.

If you can't remember to do it at first, put a bit of colored tape on your watch, phone, steering wheel, or typewriter to help remind you.

Progressive Relaxation Technique

A problem for many people who are often stressed is not knowing what it feels like to be relaxed. When they are told to slow down and take it easy, they don't understand in real physical terms what that means. The Progressive Relaxation technique[1] is designed to relax the body in progressive steps, beginning with those areas that are easiest to relax. Developed by psychophysiologist Edmund Jacobsen in the 1930s, this technique has two forms, active and passive.

The active form asks you to tense a set of muscles, hold for five to seven seconds, and then release. As you progress upward from your toes, you will clearly feel the difference between the deliberately tensed sensation and the released one. You will become more sensitive to both.

The technique's passive form also progresses slowly from one part of the body to the next. But instead of tensing the muscles, you are asked just to focus on them while you breathe deeply and thus release tension. Visualization (discussed in Chapter Nine) is easily integrated into Progressive Relaxation once the basic pattern is established. This technique — either the active or passive form — should be practiced twice a day for fifteen minutes. As Jacobsen said, "An anxious mind cannot exist within a relaxed body."

Meditation

Once breathing is regulated and the muscles are relaxed, it is time to turn the mind inward. Turning inward means that we, by conscious decision, eliminate preconception, anxiety, and activity from our thoughts. This process is meditation. Meditation does not produce lethargy, nor is it rumination over a problem. It doesn't involve or produce a lack of control. When our minds are still, we are free to experience existence in another way, separate from our thoughts.

Meditation can be part of practicing a religion, as it is in Zen, or it can be just a twenty minute time-out from daily activities. It can be best to practice before meals. Most authorities suggest dawn and dusk as the most appropriate times. In Eastern religions, the goal of meditation is to reach a state of awareness called cosmic consciousness or *satori*, where we fuse with a higher energy.

Some systems of meditation focus on an object during the sessions. Others, such as transcendental meditation, focus on a *mantra*, or word. Kundalini yoga focuses on internal sensations, and Soto Zen asks the meditator to open up to external sensations without interacting with or judging them. In all of them, the point is that it is much easier to clear the mind when there is a specific focus. All require a passive attitude and an inner receptivity to the process.

The practice of meditation receives as much emphasis as you are willing to give it. It does not replace other factors that combine to produce a healthy life. And it does not mean that other factors in your life will change. But any shift in perception will lead to changes in behavior. Realizing the importance of relaxation may lead to a reevaluation of diet, for example, or an awareness of the need for less demanding activities. And remember, the practice of meditation doesn't mean that you are a candidate for a religious or psychological cult.

One of meditation's prime benefits is that it can be more psychologically and physiologically restful than sleep. Many people feel they need less sleep when they are meditating. In meditation, the mind is truly at rest. When we sleep, however, the dream state is active — for some people, it is extremely active. They can wake up feeling more tired than when they went to bed!

Research shows that meditators have greater and more diverse responses to stress than people who don't meditate.[2] What is most important, meditators recover more quickly from fight or flight reactions. With further training, meditators can reduce the stress response so that it is less taxing to the body. A low arousal state can be repeatedly substituted until it becomes the norm. This is an effective method for lowering the pressure of everyday stress.

Thus, meditators show a greater ability to become accustomed to repeated stressors. This frees them to deal with other matters of more importance. To an extent, we all become accustomed to environmental stressors. If we must live with a noisy air conditioner, we grow used to it or tune it out. But certain stressors aren't as easily dealt with. Each of us will have a different list, but some common irritants include heavy traffic, loud neighbors, irritating co-workers or relatives, and dull or repetitive tasks. Since there's very little we can do to remove all the stressors from our lives, we must find healthy ways of incorporating them. Research also shows that the failure to habituate is an underlying factor in stress-related disorders such as high blood pressure and chronic headaches.

Meditation requires practice and patience; progress does not occur overnight. Many people stick to practicing meditation because they are very much opposed to alcohol and drugs as a means of relaxing. Somewhere deep inside, they believe meditation will work.

The experience with meditation may grow out of crisis, but can start with one very valuable asset: the willingness to look inward. In our outward-directed society, it's often very difficult to summon this willingness. We often get no support or encouragement to acquire the habit of silence. We can, however, encourage this practice in ourselves and in each other. Meditation isn't anesthesia; it's harmony.

CHAPTER 9

Relaxation and Biofeedback

This chapter presents numerous relaxation techniques designed to accomplish various goals. The purpose of a hypnotic suggestion is quite specific, for example, while autogenic exercises (which include hypnosis) are designed to produce thorough relaxation. The variety of techniques allows for freedom of choice. If meditation proves too general a technique, then visualization may help.

Many people choose a basic technique and then augment it with one or more of the others depending on circumstances. This flexibility will keep the practice of meditation vital, and yield a variety of results according to the goals you set.

The Relaxation Response

Herbert Benson's work with transcendental meditation (TM) led him to develop the relaxation response.[1] While TM practitioners felt the benefits of relaxation, Benson believed that the emphasis on a *mantra* or verbal cue, derived from Hindu, was too foreign for most Westerners to feel comfortable with. Therefore, he formulated a technique similar to TM which uses more familiar cues, such as 'one' or 'love'. This response begins by asking you to deeply relax your muscles, and, as you do so, to be aware of your breathing. Each time you exhale, silently repeat the cue. Do this for ten to twenty minutes. When you have finished, sit quietly for a few minutes, first keeping your eyes closed and then keeping them open. Use the technique twice a day.

The Quieting Response

Psychiatrist Charles Stroebel formulated a technique that can be used throughout the day. It takes about six seconds, and can effectively counteract the effects of stress. Stroebel believed that traditional twenty-minute meditation sessions are too restrictive, especially for time-urgent Type A personalities who find simply sitting still stressful. He developed a response to counteract the initial phases of the fight or flight response which seems to last about six seconds.

To practice this response, you begin by recognizing the fight or flight symptoms. At that moment, smile: this notifies the brain that you are replacing negative emotions with positive ones. Then you say to yourself, "Alert, amused mind — calm body." This reinforces the positive message to the brain. Similar positive cues are sent as you breathe deeply, making sure more oxygen gets to the brain. Be aware of how much tension you are carrying in your jaw, tongue, and shoulders — common areas of tension — and release it. Go back to your normal activities. This response takes about six months of practice before it becomes automatic. But, when used 50 to 100 times a day, it can produce a marked increase in relaxation.

Autogenic Training

German psychiatrist Johannes Schultz found through his clinical experience with hypnosis that patients felt warmth and heaviness while hypnotized. Incorporating these sensations, he combined techniques of autohypnosis with specific exercises to induce a state of deep relaxation. Autogenic training differs from meditation in that the exercises focus on physical sensations. Using a series of steps, the technique seeks to produce (1) heaviness in the limbs; (2) warmth in the extremities; (3) cardiac regulation; (4) slowed respiration; (5) warmth in the abdominal region (focusing on the solar plexis); and (6) a cool forehead. Each step is practiced until the particular sensation is repeatedly achieved before the next step is taken.

The technique can take from two months to a year to master. At that point, the sensations can be achieved in two to four minutes. Three sessions are recommended a day: after lunch, after dinner, and before going to bed. In the beginning, it is important to practice in a quiet environment and to use a position (sitting or lying down) which reduces muscle tension to a minimum. After the steps are mastered, however, the technique can be practiced in the office, on a bus, or anyplace. This technique will work best for highly motivated people who have a reasonable degree of self-direction and concentration. Masters in autogenic training can control a wide range of functions, even to the point of self-induced anesthesia.

Self-hypnosis
Self-hypnosis is a goal-oriented technique you can use to produce relaxation as well as to bring about desired behavioral changes. The trance has some similarities to the meditative state, including increased alpha wave activity, and lowered heart rate, blood pressure, and respiration.

After relaxing the muscles and breathing deeply, you repeat positive statements aimed at achieving behavioral changes, such as, "I will exercise every other day," or "I am an attractive, worthwhile person." It's important to remember that positive statements rather than negative ones will produce the changes more successfully. The subconscious prefers to hear good things about us. It can, however, focus on negativity.

This technique is also effective for breaking down fear. For example, going to the dentist, driving across bridges or on the freeway, or flying can be terrifying experiences. Positive hypnotic suggestions can be very helpful.

How It's Done
These instructions will give you a better idea of how autosuggestion or self-hypnosis works:

1. As with meditation, find a quiet place to sit or lie down. Lower the lights or turn them off. Loosen restrictive clothing and remove your shoes. Close your eyes.

2. Take a deep breath, exhaling fully and slowly. Continue to breath slowly and deeply, letting all your worries and anxieties slip away. Your thoughts are like feathers — you are aware of them, but they are weightless and move effortlessly away from you. Let them float by. You are more relaxed with every breath. Your mind is becoming blank.

3. Beginning with your toes, release the tension in your muscles as you exhale. Let it all go. As you move up your body, release the tension in your calves, thighs, buttocks, and abdomen. There is no timetable for this: just let it go. Continue up your rib cage, chest, shoulders, and arms — and down to your fingertips. Relax your neck, your scalp, and the muscles in your face. Continue to breathe slowly. Relax. Your muscles feel very heavy and warm. Repeat to yourself: "I am more and more relaxed. My body feels very, very heavy." Feel the heaviness. Feel the warmth.

4. You are now entering an elevator on the twentieth floor of a building. As the elevator slowly descends, you become more relaxed. Count to yourself: twenty, nineteen, eighteen, seventeen . . . and breathe deeply at each floor. You are becoming more and more peaceful and relaxed. Enjoy the ride. When you arrive at the ground floor, you are very relaxed and comfortable.

5. You will now count backward from thirty to zero (it helps to visualize the numbers as you say them). While you do this, continue to breathe deeply, knowing that when you reach zero, you will be in a highly receptive state. You will be ready to receive some positive suggestions. Take your time.

6. Each suggestion is repeated six times. Here are some optional suggestions:

   "I am a valuable and worthwhile person."

   "I feel mature, confident, and assertive."

   "I am happy, energetic, and outgoing."

   "I am becoming more aware of my positive traits."

   "I am becoming more physically, mentally, and spiritually healthy."

"I am more relaxed, calm, and alert."

"I will sleep soundly."

"I am improving my eating and exercise habits."

"Each time I practice meditation, I will become more deeply relaxed."

Note: Any other goals can be included gradually. But be sure the statements are positive. Instead of saying, "I won't overeat anymore," try, "I will eat what I need to maintain my proper weight."

7. It is now time to come back to an alert state. Get back on the elevator, and begin to count forward as the elevator rises to the twentieth floor. It ascends slowly and smoothly, and you enjoy the ride going up as much as you did going down. Continue to breathe slowly. When the doors open at the top, open your eyes and stretch. You are now refreshed and alert.

Self-hypnosis works best with regular practice. Consider it like vitamins: you need a steady dose to get the most benefit. Even if this is not one of your goals, you will find yourself calmer and more relaxed from regular use.

Visualization

Visualization is the "summoning and holding of certain images in the mind for examining and exploration of their effects on consciousness."[2]

Typically, visualization is used with other techniques: deep breathing, progressive muscle relaxation, the early stages of autogenic training, or all of these.

When meditators are relaxed and ready to focus attention on particular images, they might begin with a color that occupies the entire field. Depending on how they feel, they might focus on blues and greens to enhance a feeling of coolness, or they might choose reds and yellows to enhance warmth. They might then visualize simple movement such as a cloud drifting across the sky. Then they put the colors and movements together. These simple exercises prepare the mind for more complex visualizations, a necessary phase for people who are not particularly visual in everyday life.

How It's Done

The following instructions will give you an idea of exactly how this technique works:

1. As with meditation, go to a quiet corner or room, away from noise. Turn down the lights. Get into a comfortable position, and loosen restrictive clothing. Remove your shoes. Close your eyes.

2. Take a slow, deep breath. Hold it for a moment, and then slowly and completely exhale. Continue to breathe deeply, allowing the anxiety and tension to slip from you. Any thoughts or worries can slip away with each deep breath. It's all right to be aware of your thoughts, but let them go. Pretend they are feathers floating through your mind.

3. Visualize a warm, heavy feeling in your muscles. Beginning with your toes, focus on your muscles. With each exhale, let the tension in your toes slip away. As you progress up your body, from feet to calves to thighs to abdomen and buttocks, continue to breathe deeply and release the tension. Continue to your rib cage, your chest, your shoulders, and down your arms to your fingertips. Continue with your neck, your scalp, your face: release all the tension in the muscles until you are completely relaxed.

4. Each of us has a special place where we feel peaceful. It might be somewhere we've traveled, or right in our backyard. It might be a place in our childhood, or somewhere we're dreaming about going. Visualize that place. Be aware of everything about it: the colors, textures, smells, and sounds. If you have no particular place in mind, use this one:

   Imagine that you are outdoors on a calm, beautiful spring day. The sun is shining down on you, warming your arms and legs, bathing your face in lovely soft light. You are strolling through a meadow filled with wild flowers swaying gently in the breeze. Birds sing sweetly in the trees. You feel totally relaxed and accepted here. This is your place. All of your worries and thoughts are insignificant as you enjoy this little vacation from them. This phase should last from ten to twenty minutes where you simply bask in the peace and quiet.

5. When you are ready, take several full, deep breaths to prepare for your return to an alert state. With each breath, say to yourself, "I am becoming more and more alert. I am refreshed and relaxed." When you are ready, open your eyes and stretch.

Note: These mini-vacations can last from five to twenty minutes once you're comfortable with the process. They can be used at work during breaks in the shorter form, and at home after your workday is over, or whenever you need to relax. The more often you visualize, the more real the environment becomes and the deeper the relaxation you experience.

The More Advanced Steps

Subsequent steps with visualization involve focusing on a particular object and holding it. That's followed by sessions in which a concept such as love or happiness evokes particular images. If the image is disturbing, meditators are given a cancellation formula that brings them to a lighter state of relaxation. They then return to focus on a different image: they imagine themselves in a scene — at the beach, or soaring above the mountains — followed by the introduction of other people into the picture.

They move from imagining neutral people in their lives to the inclusion of significant others. The goal is to discover insight about these relationships and to alter the person's perception about them. This stage should be done with the help of a trained facilitator.

For people who choose not to use the technique to the advanced levels, visualization can still be used in various ways. It can:

- induce a meditative state as its primary focus;
- be used with other techniques to deepen relaxation or awareness;
- stimulate the creative imagination;

- mobilize the body's defenses against disease;
- break the pattern of prolonged stress;
- provide a release from states of hyperarousal;
- promote healing;
- restore a sense of self-control and thus produce a more positive outlook; and
- help to manage pain.

Visualization in Healing

The work of O. Carl Simonton and Stephanie Matthews-Simonton with cancer patients has dramatized the value of visualization.[3] The Simontons found that there is a direct relationship between patients' positive attitudes toward life and how well they respond to treatment. The belief system of patients, their families, significant friends, and their physicians are all important in how well the patient responds to treatment.

Going on the assumption that positive attitudes can be taught, the Simontons developed a system for evaluating and training their patients. The goal was to maximize treatment by relying heavily on visualization. This is how it worked:

The patient was taught to focus on his or her breathing, to relax, and then to visualize a pleasant scene such as a mountain meadow or lakeshore. Then the patient visualized his or her illness in a way that was meaningful, perhaps as an army of black knights or menacing aliens. This was followed by visualizing his or her treatment, normally radiation or chemotherapy, or a combination of both, also in a dramatic way. The patient then imagined an army of white blood cells carrying the dead cancer cells out through the blood or lungs. Finally, the patient visualized cancer mortally wounded in some way — shrinking or evaporating like the wicked witch in *The Wizard of Oz*.

Patients reported gaining a profound sense of communication with their bodies, as well a needed feeling of control over the disease and their lives. As a boost to the medical regimen of these patients, visualization played a vital role in recovery. Their bodies responded to the images as if they were real. Several factors contributed to the success of the images: (1) patients had to want to get better (or to remain healthy); (2) they had to relax because tension will block the images; (3) their visualization needed to be positive, with positive verbal cues; and (4) they needed to imagine immediate positive results, using the present tense and specific goals.[4]

Family Participation

Members of the same family can use visualization together. Let's take the example of two sisters. When one was diagnosed with Hodgkin's disease several years ago, the other sister participated in the ill sister's treatment with a combination of meditation, prayer, and visualization. The ill sister also learned to visualize. Together they worked on the illness until it was in remission — it is now, five years later, virtually accepted as cured. Although both women agree that the visualization was important, they do not suggest it as the sole treatment.

Yoga

Yoga has been a part of Indian culture for thousands of years, and there are many forms that emphasize various aspects of yoga. The goal of yoga is the integration of mind and body, and our control over both. Practice will lead to the highest level of attainment — an altered state of consciousness called *samadhi*, where the mind fuses with the universe.

Yoga is also a system of living. It has prescribed dietary guidelines as well as a philosophy for treating illness. This is based on the belief that the body is self-regulating, and if provided with a favorable environment, will return to balance. Our job is to provide this environment.

Through a series of positions, or *asanas*, the body relaxes and the mind focuses inward. Many people find relief from stress in practicing a combination of *asanas*, or in *asanas* plus meditation. Classes on yoga are widely available, and are very helpful for those who need the support of a group in learning new techniques. Yoga, like most meditation techniques, requires frequent sessions to derive the greatest benefit.

Desensitization

Traumatic experiences in our past, especially in childhood, often cause phobias. Fear of flying, fear of being in enclosed spaces, fear of snakes or spiders are common. But nearly anything can be the focus of a phobia. The possibility of facing a fearful situation can cause everything from vague feelings of uneasiness to anxiety attacks. The result is that we alter our lives in some way to avoid the fearful situation. Sometimes avoiding situations isn't enough, however, since simply imagining the event can set off an attack. Our bodies respond as if the image in our minds was real.

Desensitization is a technique for removing the fear. It was developed by behaviorist Joseph Wolpe, and is a form of reprogramming the mind. The technique is comprised of a series of steps of which relaxation is an essential prerequisite. Persons must be able to tell whether or not they are becoming tense. Then, the fearful event is approached step by step.

Whenever people feel tension mounting, they can go back to a more relaxing point and remain there, focusing on breathing and releasing tension. In this way they progress until they can imagine themselves in fearful situations without panic. Then they will be ready to test the waters and confront their fears. There will be stress in facing the situation, but through desensitization people will be able to cope with it.

Another type of desensitization is called *in vivo* desensitization. In it, people act out the steps until they are comfortable. William Masters and Virginia Johnson use this technique for sexual dysfunction.

For those people suffering from more common phobias, desensitization groups are available. Clients are able to conquer their fears under the guidance of a trained therapist, as well as share the progress (and expense) with others. For less common phobias, or for people who wish to reprogram privately, individual sessions can be arranged.

Biofeedback

Biofeedback is a procedure that uses electrical instruments to measure physiological functions, and then displays these functions in easily observable ways. In a typical session, the client is hooked up to equipment that can display heart rate, body temperature, level of muscle tension, brain wave pattern, and other physiological information.

Patients are instructed to slow a flashing light or steady a needle point, and are often given relaxing sentences or images to help do it. It doesn't matter how patients prompt changes in the tone or light; it matters that it is done. The result is a state of relaxation that the patients see and feel. Once patients see or hear the differences in their heart rate, it is easier for them to reproduce the effect later.

Similarities between biofeedback training and other relaxation techniques are obvious. Clients attend sessions in quiet, comfortable settings with a minimum of distractions. Again, the passive attitude is critical. Clients learn to allow the changes to take place by focusing their attention. Unlike traditional meditation, however, electronic equipment is the guide. Clients are rewarded with knowing exactly when and how they become relaxed.

If we look at our disorders as disturbances that indicate a system out of balance, then through biofeedback we can tap into the nervous system and help correct it. We can speak directly to our bodies and thus break the stress response. Biofeedback is particularly helpful for specific stress-related problems such as migraine headaches, high blood pressure, asthma, or muscle tension. It is also used to treat chronic pain.

Inherent in the biofeedback process are three assumptions: (1) each change in the body is accompanied by a conscious or unconscious change in the mental and emotional state; (2) deep relaxation allows patients to become aware of their feelings and thoughts; and (3) any biological or neurological function capable of being monitored can be controlled if patients have enough information about it.

Biofeedback is uniquely suited to our lifestyle in the United States. Looking inward, which is the basis of all relaxation techniques, is not something most of us are comfortable with — it's not part of our attitude toward life. To reflect on our heartbeat or the temperature of our hands and feet is not a widely accepted activity. Yet for the few minutes we are hooked up to machinery in a biofeedback lab, that is our job. We get objective information from a piece of equipment appropriate for a culture fascinated with technology. And there's no waiting for results. They are in front of us every moment we're in the session.

Beyond these factors, why do we need machines to tell us how we feel? When the machine talks back to us, the evidence is hard to ignore. Some might say: "Oh, so that's what they mean by alpha waves!" The act of interpreting, of matching up the information with our actual experience, is critical because no one feels tension or relaxation exactly the same way. The equipment is a handy navigational device that can speed the process of inner awareness.

How Did They Figure This Out?

After World War I, a German scientist named Hans Berger discovered the existence of two types of brain waves. His research involved hooking up clients to an electroencephalogram, or EEG machine. Electrodes were attached to a person's scalp and connected to a monitor, or brain wave amplifier, which was also hooked to a recorder. During the sessions, the brain waves sent out electric impulses that were then displayed on the recorder as a continuously moving line.[5]

The two types of waves that appeared most frequently Berger called *alpha* and *beta*. He also related them to specific mental states. Alpha waves were produced when his clients were not concentrating on anything in particular, while beta waves appeared when his clients were problem-solving. Since then, two more types of brain waves have been discovered. *Theta waves* are usually produced during fantasies or hallucinations. *Delta waves* occur almost always during sleep.

Scientists believe that the waves are produced by electrochemical activity in the brain cells. The job of this activity is to transmit information throughout the body; when electrochemical activity fires in a rhythmic pattern, waves are formed. The brain rarely produces the same type of wave from each hemisphere: the right side may be producing alpha, while the left side may be producing beta.[6]

In the late 1950s, Dr. Joe Kamiya developed equipment that was capable of turning brain waves, as measured by the EEG machine, into a tone. Each time one of his clients produced say, an alpha wave, the client would hear a corresponding tone. When the client stopped producing that wave, the tone would stop too. Kamiya's clients were asked to produce specific tones as long as possible, regardless of how they did it. Once trained to produce alpha in this way, Dr. Kamiya's clients could then produce alpha away from the equipment as well. The technique of biofeedback was born.[7]

At the Menninger Foundation in Kansas a decade later, Elmer and Alyce Green's work integrated biofeedback and autogenic training.[8] Their volunteers were asked to do three things at once: reduce muscle tension in their right arms, increase the alpha waves they were producing, and raise the temperature in their right hands. They were hooked up to appropriate biofeedback machinery that gave them information about each function. And they were given standard autogenic relaxation phrases such as — "My hands are heavy and warm" — to repeat during the sessions.

The Greens found that volunteers could learn to relax with biofeedback training much faster than with autogenic training alone. Some biofeedback volunteers learned in twenty minutes what took autogenic training volunteers four to six months to learn.

Also, the Greens are credited with discovering the use of biofeedback in the treatment of specific disorders. This happened by accident. One of the women who was participating in the studies came in with a migraine headache. During her session she recovered, and the Greens, sensing a new direction in their work, began to investigate.

One of the most common complaints of migraine sufferers is cold hands and feet. This is because part of the nervous system is overreacting, causing the constriction of arteries inside the brain as well as extreme dilation of arteries in the scalp. The Greens reasoned that if migraine sufferers could be taught via biofeedback to warm their extremities (again, using the autogenic training cues), then they might find relief without the use of drugs and painkillers. Many physicians now refer migraine sufferers to biofeedback clinics, and some insurance companies will cover part of the cost.

Finally, does biofeedback mean that people are hooked up to machines forever? The answer is an emphatic no. Clients are trained in a center, either alone or with others, with the goal of becoming self-regulating when they are ready. This can take a very short time, or longer, depending on the individual and the situation. Once people are trained in the technique, it is no longer necessary for them to receive the feedback; they can do it themselves. But there are portable units available. In either case, the homework is the same: one or two twenty minute sessions a day.

As a beginning, biofeedback offers some distinct advantages to people who wish to control their stress levels. But biofeedback for the treatment of a specific disorder is not an end in itself. Once the headaches or asthma or irregular heartbeats are brought under control, it is time to integrate relaxation techniques into our lives on a permanent basis. This can be done using various techniques or relying on one. The object is to retain communication with the body, and to foster its natural inclination toward balance.

Just a Little Peace and Quiet

Instead of quick cures advertised on television, we are suggesting a very different approach. We hope you've found among these techniques one that you feel comfortable fitting into your life, one that provides not only the method but the meaning to make practice and patience worthwhile. The healing sound, the comforting image, the essential silence that enables us to break the stress response is a precious addition to lives too full of noise and activity.

CHAPTER 10

Purpose and Meaning

Throughout this book we have talked about reducing stress through self-awareness, acceptance, and planning. We believe that people's reactions will become more positive when they acknowledge that change is inevitable, and that they are capable of handling it in a healthy way. This increases their confidence, and they will feel more at ease. When people live less anxiously, they reduce the risk of physical and psychological breakdowns and relapse.

At times we feel baffled, even overwhelmed, by what is happening to us. Events occur that defy our ability to come to grips with them. We can't foresee or prepare for many of the crises that arise. When tragedy happens, for example, we might think we are unable to stop the suffering of ourselves or those we love. We might want to shake our fists at God and rage: Why? Why me?

When we come up against these walls, we must look inside for the proper resources to adapt. We have to stretch ourselves into new shapes to find the right solution. It's likely that our vision of ourselves and the world will change. These are times when we question our beliefs: we are testing them against what we experience. The subsequent overhaul, even if the adjustment is minor, brings values and experience closer together. Thus, we become more integrated, another term for *mature*. This is a process that requires no degree or title. We are all capable of reaching inside ourselves for the values that sustain us.

When we examine our values, we are examining our spirituality. Stress management is incomplete without this process. If we know how we fit in the great scheme of things, we can relax. We have a sense of purpose. No matter how difficult our path, our beliefs can carry us through.

This is especially relevant in recovery. In the Twelve Step program, the First Step is a big one: In Alcoholics Anonymous, it says, "We admitted we were powerless over alcohol — that our lives had become unmanageable." This is surrender, but it is far from hopeless. Step Two states, "Came to believe that a Power greater than ourselves could restore us to sanity." After surrender comes belief — faith. Step Three continues, "Made a decision to turn our will and our lives over to the care of God *as we understood Him*." This is a transformation born of desperation and self-destruction. Like the phoenix, we rise from the ashes of addiction into a new life.

Belief in the Higher Power and the Twelve Step program sustains us through those many months and years of change as we develop healthy living skills. At first it may seem arbitrary: we've been down so long, any change looks good. The more we work the program, however, the more success we feel. Our faith grows stronger, and we are anchored by it.

In this chapter we will discuss spirituality more completely. It is the key to stress management. We'll use the theories of Carl Rogers, Rollo May, and M. Scott Peck to explain how values and spirituality function in our lives. We'll also discuss the relationship between religion and faith.

Where Can I Find Meaning?

We live in an age characterized by anxiety. Through advanced communications, we are privy to the conflicts and suffering of people around the globe. In our homes on television we see the effects of war, famine, disease, and social unrest. We carry with us the knowledge that at any moment we could annihilate ourselves through the use of nuclear weapons. Our future appears as unstable as the present.

Hardly anyone believes that we live in the best of all possible worlds. This considerably complicates whatever problems or challenges we face as individuals. Many people cope by ignoring the seriousness of the situation. Others are obsessed by it. Some people escape into the past or fantasize about the future. Some struggle to do the best job they can with what they have. Most of us do all of these things. In what seems like pitifully small doses, we gain wisdom. Wisdom comes from self-awareness. By solving our problems, we find meaning.[1]

We begin to know ourselves through our relationship with the world. When we, through our experience, have developed beliefs that reflect who we actually are, we are mature. We can't adopt a set of values from other people, no matter how attractive they may look. Our values must be as unique as we are — even though we may share them with others. Until we have tested them against our own lives, they aren't ours. Our values enable us to take responsibility for our behavior and to learn from it. The more we believe in what we do, the more meaningful our lives will be.

How Do Values Develop?

Our values are determined by the age we live in. We get them initially from the group we're born into: the family, the community, the society. We have a wide range of choice within American society. But it would be unlikely that children could grow up with, say, Swedish values in the U.S. even though their parents are of Swedish heritage. Similarly, children with a Renaissance outlook in the twentieth century would find themselves bewildered. Because we change with the times, part of the challenge of developing a belief system is to stay aware of the world.[2]

We regard group values as our own, whether we recognize this or not. This means we normally look outside of ourselves to find the values that cause us to be loved and accepted. As adults, we realize that being what the group approves of is not always what we as individuals need. Thus, we adjust those values according to who we are. For most of us, this is a continual process of reconciliation: we must find a balance between the acceptance we need from others with the desire to become self-actualized.

In uncertain times, group values tend to become more traditional and conservative. This is because we often look to the past for tried-and-true methods of handling change. This can make us feel more secure, providing us with a bulwark against the tumultuous events happening around us. Conservative approaches to solving problems, however, can lead to dogmatic thinking — the "right" and "wrong" that enables us to deny the validity of other philosophies, races, or the opposite sex. It shuts down our creativity in coping with the unexpected. If these values are upheld as untestable, then we will feel the difference between what we believe in and what we're actually going through — a very stressful situation! Of course, we need to feel safe. But, safety should not be the only goal in our lives.

We make decisions about the world as mature adults in much the same way as infants do. Infants trust themselves first; their needs and desires truly reflect who they are. They are not concerned with attaining the approval of others. Their expectations are their own. Infants will always choose to promote themselves; therefore, their values are flexible, and they function in the present. They are able to take advantage of new situations — a new toy, new position, new skills are all put to use for their benefit.[3]

Likewise, mature people have integrated their values and their experiences, and they know who they are. They are different from other people, and different, though part of, the group. If their beliefs dictate that they stand against the group, they will do so because they know that to back down will not be in their best interest. They, too, live in the present, evaluating circumstances as they arise in order to make beneficial choices. Thus, they are flexible and creative in new situations. This is not an easy way to live. But it is a meaningful way to live, the more so if they are truly committed to growth.

How Do I Get There from Here?

Carl Rogers offers the following "value directions" for developing a mature set of beliefs.

- Move away from facades.
- Move away from "oughts" and "shoulds."
- Move away from meeting expectations.
- Move away from fixed goals.
- Move toward self-direction.
- Move toward self-worth.
- Move toward valuing both inner and outer experiences — what we feel as well as what others feel.
- Move toward sensitivity and acceptance of others (we appreciate people for who they are).
- Move toward developing deep relationships.[4]

Fundamental Skill: Discipline

The process of solving our problems is a hard one. It frequently involves pain and suffering — two experiences we'd like to do without. To follow through, therefore, we need discipline. According to psychiatrist M. Scott Peck, four tools can be used in developing discipline:

- delaying gratification;
- accepting responsibility;
- dedicating yourself to the truth; and
- balancing.[5]

1. We delay gratification when we schedule our pain and pleasure to get pain out of the way first so we can enjoy the pleasure more fully. We eat our vegetables before the ice cream, run errands before playing racquetball, and buy Christmas presents before opening our own on Christmas morning. As we grow up, we develop a sense of what is right for us to delay. At some point, it may be more important to eat the ice cream first. We may throw caution to the wind and loaf all day instead of paying bills and making phone calls. As a rule, however, we use delayed gratification as a means of planning for and achieving goals.

2. We need to accept responsibility for a problem before we can solve it. This is difficult because in doing so we are likely to be uncomfortable and possibly in pain. When we accept the consequences of our behavior, we are opening ourselves up to punishment or feelings of shame or failure. It is common to deny responsibility, to shove it onto someone else. Unfortunately, in doing so, we give away the power we have to use our freedom. We then feel that nothing we do is of consequence. Self-esteem is based on acknowledging that we are responsible for our actions. If not, we remain children.

3. By truth, we mean reality. We aren't born understanding or facing up to the world around us. We have to grow, test ourselves, and explore before we "know" reality. As we change, our vision of reality changes. We take on newer and more difficult responsibilities, and experience more complex problems that influence our outlook. Because we know ourselves in relation to the world, we must keep exploring and changing our vision. This means foregoing comfortable notions about ourselves as "right" or "perfect." It means challenging what we believe.

4. Balancing is a process of choosing which people, events, and ideas we plan to spend time and attention on. It is a factor in being disciplined because it means stepping back to take an inventory of our lives. We may find that some parts of our lives are out of balance: we spend too much time at work, worry too much about our children, or neglect our playful selves. Balancing is choosing a variety of activities and beliefs that are meaningful to us. Again, it is easier to slip into routines that dictate to us the balance of our lives rather than to rework them into a more satisfying whole. Balancing requires thought, and constant evaluation to make sure that we are living the life best suited for us.

Fundamental Skill: Courage

Rollo May states that "Courage is the basic virtue for everyone so long as he continues to grow, to move ahead.[6] We need courage to confront our problems, to make decisions that challenge us. We all long to remain in comfortable nooks and to protect ourselves from difficulty. When we are threatened, our tendency is to run the other way. Unfortunately, our problems follow us and eventually overtake us. When we act in a cowardly way, it is generally because we fear rejection by others. Isolation is considered worse punishment than loss of self-esteem. But, most of us find that this is untrue.

It takes courage to form deep relationships because it's a risk to both give and to receive love. It takes courage to put our plans into action, and to stick with them during times of frustration or delay. We may be asked to be courageous not only for ourselves but for others in very difficult circumstances. But more likely, we will have many opportunities during the day to make courageous choices. This can be anything from speaking to a neighbor about his barking dog to giving someone a lift home when it takes us out of our way. Courage is required to live up to our commitments. Courage is required to grow. This kind of growth enables us to become more confident and more assured of our ability to make healthy choices. In this way, we avoid living in the shadow of fear.

Fundamental Skill: The Ability to Love

The ability to love requires self-awareness. To love others, we must be sympathetic to them. We must care about their thoughts and feelings. Love also requires that we know who we are, and that we are separate from our lovers. This means that we are free to be ourselves, just as the other person is free. Dependence is not love.

It is a paradox that we grow when we have as our goal the growth of others. Nevertheless, when we take to heart the best interests of our loved ones, we are opening ourselves up to change. As we watch them struggle to become mature, we may feel tension, doubt, and pain. It takes great courage to let go, but, in another paradox, the more freedom inside the relationship, the more committed the partners can be.

Commitment is the foundation of loving relationships. Especially in marriage, the partners need to know that they can struggle to resolve the issues that arise without fear of breaking up. If we don't believe this, then there is little incentive to resolve the issues. We are unlikely to put much time or energy into a marriage without commitment.

Love requires that we move away from laziness. Love is work, and asks us to be courageous and responsible in our actions. To live a loving life, we have to confront our fears. This always involves risk. The more lovingly we live, the more risk is involved. But, happily, we also derive greater meaning and satisfaction.

One of the simplest and yet most difficult ways to show love is to listen. We seem to go out of our way to avoid listening to others. Yet we demand that others listen to us! We can keep from listening by forbidding conversation, or simply by refusing to listen to what other people say. We can listen selectively or just pretend to listen until it is our turn to talk again. To truly listen, however, is an act of love. To do this requires that we suspend our internal dialogue, our plans, our expectations, our judgments, and frame of reference, and try — as much as we can — to hear with our hearts. This is a gift to someone else, but it is a gift to ourselves as well. In these moments we learn a great deal. Listening is an excellent skill to develop, and most of us have ample opportunity to practice it.

Finally, when we choose to love a person, a group, or an idea, we choose to be fully alive. This is not easy, and yet it is mature. Our values reach fruition in a life based on love. Love is self-replenishing. When we behave lovingly toward others with no thought to reward, love comes back to us many times over.

Fundamental Skill: Living in the Present

Time is not just the seconds measured off the clock, but the meaning of what we are going through. Time often passes quickly when we enjoy ourselves; it drags when we are depressed or in pain. The more we consciously direct our lives, the more constructively we can use time. This means living in the present, utilizing what's available to us now. We bring the weight of our past and our dreams of the future to bear when we confront the reality of the present; they enrich our experience. But, neither past nor future is an escape or excuse.

Problem-solving takes time. Most of us have trouble acknowledging that. When we want to avoid pain, we don't take the time necessary to truly solve our problems. Unfortunately, there's no way around it; what we don't fully resolve will stay with us until we do. The key to successful resolution is dealing with the person we are now — not the person we were, or the person we think we are going to be. Both past and future are beyond our control, but that hardly makes us powerless. By choosing to deal with events in the present, we strengthen our self-concept as well as our control over time. The best defense against an uncertain future is to live fully each moment as it comes.

Fundamental Skill: Spirituality

Many of us question the paradox of life, and want to know whether or not there is a God. We want to understand the universe, the nature of humanity, and our relationship to other living things. We strive to realize our dreams; yet, considering that we all die, we might wonder what it's all for. Because we have intelligence and curiosity, we struggle to provide ourselves with a framework to answer these questions. This contemplation of meaning is part of our spirituality. Faith provides us with the motivation to confront our problems. If we don't believe that things will improve through our efforts, we will make no effort. We will retire from life and simply wait to die.

Just as our bodies develop when we use them, our spirituality develops when we put it into action. Through contemplation, prayer, and meditation we start listening to our inner voices, which give us direction. This is communication with God, of a life force, of a Higher Power. Although not widely condoned in our culture, this communication is a vital part of self-realization. Again, because this is a journey into the unknown, we are risking ourselves; we don't know what's out there. This may provoke some anxiety — enough to turn away from it. But like other risks, the rewards can outweigh the fear.

The Reward Is Inner Peace: Serenity

The search for serenity is a lonely path, for there are no compatriots. A few people serve us as teachers, but even they can't come with us. The further we travel, the less we feel ourselves as entities, and the more we feel akin to all other living things. Time ceases to define us. Death ceases to terrify us. We experience freedom, joy, and profound peace of mind. There is no longer the need to struggle with life as though climbing a steep mountain. Instead, we see that we are necessary in the great scheme, and that our lives are the microcosm and macrocosm of life itself. In losing ourselves, we gain knowledge of a greater whole. Though most of us choose to leave this side of our lives unexplored until crisis forces us into it, we have within us the capacity for great awareness.

Spiritual awakening is one of the most profound experiences we are likely to have. It touches every aspect of our lives, and alters our self-concept as well as our vision of reality. Generally — and we're speaking very generally — this involves an experience where our normal framework doesn't function. For example, someone we love may have died tragically. The use of alcohol or other drugs to deaden pain doesn't work anymore. Or, an event, which seems like a miracle, saves us from death or injury. Or, we may have reached the breaking point in a long struggle and have no other coping skills. In opening our hearts to what we don't understand, our spirituality is awakened.

This is a time when our lives are governed by faith, pure and simple. This can be both freeing and frightening at the same time. We are free because we, as humans, are not the ultimate power and we're not in control of everything. It's frightening because we have reached the limits of our understanding and knowledge. We don't really know what's out there, and it doesn't look as if we're going to find out.

Through developing positive self-beliefs, we can find a way to reconcile the freedom and the fear. All of us have a set of beliefs, whether they are formally acknowledged beliefs or not, or whether we are fully aware of them or not. The rituals we choose to practice may be formal and institutionalized. They could just as easily be unique and unstructured. We might practice our beliefs in the company of others or alone. The bulk of our awareness may reside in a Twelve Step group; it could just as easily reside in a book of meditations and regular times of contemplation. What our beliefs do for us is meet our needs for safety and, when related to groups, acceptance. They provide the firm foundation from which we manage our freedom.

A Catholic may invest great meaning in regularly taking communion. Over and over he does exactly the same thing. This experience is comforting; he feels exactly what he expects to feel: healed.

A Buddhist may find great release in practicing chants that lead her into meditative states. In saying the ancient verses, she makes her intentions clear, thus preparing herself for a spiritual journey.

Someone else, who belongs to a Twelve Step group, may restore himself with a walk in the country on a familiar track of ground unchanged and deeply satisfying. This time alone may enable him to face life with creativity and courage.

It is also possible to find inner peace from a long period of aerobic exercise. Many long distance runners report feeling spiritually enriched after a run. In the practice of the ritual, whether it is the repetition of prayer or a long run, we meet our need to feel secure and connected to the larger world.

This, then, enables us to go on and confront the freedom that faith offers us. Most of us believe in the higher ideals: justice, integrity, truth, and compassion. It is our responsibility to live these ideals as fully as we can. So, as we choose to grow, we come closer to these goals. We risk inner conflict and, sometimes, pain in the process. When we falter, we come back and restore ourselves in affirming our beliefs.

Once we have had a spiritual awakening, we are likely to find that, instead of having things explained for us, more things happen that seem extraordinary. There are moments when we instinctively know what to do even though it may not be what we usually do: We take an alternate route home and find that there was a massive freeway pile-up on our regular route. We walk into an unfamiliar house and feel we've been there before. We exhaust our funds on monthly bills, and the next day an unexpected check arrives in the mail.

These moments, which are quite common, are times when we feel the grace of a Higher Power. According to Dr. Peck, these are moments that "serve to nurture and enhance human life and growth."[7] Though we don't completely understand them, we know they are beneficial to us. They are the times when we thank our lucky stars, or a guardian angel, or a fairy godmother, or fate, for intervening. Sometimes these moments are nothing short of miraculous.

When we look at it from this standpoint, we may not hear the voice of God as Moses did, but we can all feel the hand of God working in our lives. These fortunate moments can make us feel that we do matter in the great scheme of things. When we believe that our efforts matter, that we have the capacity to benefit ourselves and humankind, then we have developed the framework for tackling our problems. This doesn't mean we won't be baffled at times, but our problems will never defeat us. At long last, we are equal to the task.

Spirituality and Stress Management
When we feel that our lives have purpose and meaning, it is possible to make positive choices, even though they involve much time and effort. Recovery is such a choice. Faith in a Higher Power, in a Twelve Step program, and in our efforts to improve our lives serve as a buffer against stress.

This is not an easy path. It is not painless. You don't have to like the process, but you probably will like the results. Remember, you are not alone. You can do it. Follow your spiritual direction.

THE TWELVE STEPS OF A.A.*

1. We admitted we were powerless over alcohol — that our lives had become unmanageable.
2. Came to believe that a Power greater than ourselves could restore us to sanity.
3. Made a decision to turn our will and our lives over to the care of God *as we understood Him.*
4. Made a searching and fearless moral inventory of ourselves.
5. Admitted to God, to ourselves, and to another human being the exact nature of our wrongs.
6. Were entirely ready to have God remove all these defects of character.
7. Humbly asked Him to remove our shortcomings.
8. Made a list of all persons we had harmed, and became willing to make amends to them all.
9. Made direct amends to such people wherever possible, except when to do so would injure them or others.
10. Continued to take personal inventory and when we were wrong promptly admitted it.
11. Sought through prayer and meditation to improve our conscious contact with God *as we understood Him,* praying only for knowledge of His will for us and the power to carry that out.
12. Having had a spiritual awakening as the result of these steps, we tried to carry this message to alcoholics, and to practice these principles in all our affairs.

---

*The Twelve Steps are from *Alcoholics Anonymous* (Third Edition), published by A.A. World Services, Inc., New York, N.Y., pp. 59-60. Reprinted with permission.

NOTES

Chapter One: Stress
[1]Hans Selye, *Stress Without Distress* (New York: J.B. Lippincott, 1974), p. 14.
[2]Ibid., pp. 25-29.
[3]Kenneth Pelletier, *Mind As Healer, Mind As Slayer* (New York: Dell, 1977), p. 4.

Chapter Two: Hostility
[1]Meyer Friedman and Ray Rosenman, *Type A Behavior and Your Heart* (New York: Alfred A. Knopf, 1974), p. 69.
[2]Ibid., pp. 69-84.
[3]Ibid., pp. 84-96.
[4]Ibid., p. 84.
[5]Merlene Miller, Terence T. Gorski, and David K. Miller, *Learning to Live Again* (Independence, Mo.: Independence Press, 1982), pp. 196-197.
[6]Gayle Rosellini and Mark Worden, *Of Course You're Angry* (Center City, Minn.: Hazelden Educational Materials, 1985), p. 81.
[7]Ibid., p. 83.
[8]M. Scott Peck, *The Road Less Traveled* (New York: Simon and Schuster, 1978), pp. 314-316.

Chapter Four: Relapse
[1]Terence T. Gorski and Merlene Miller, *Staying Sober: A Guide for Relapse Prevention* (Independence, Mo.: Independence Press, 1986), p. 57.
[2]Ibid., p. 58.
[3]Ibid., p. 69.
[4]Ibid., pp. 71-72.
[5]Ibid., pp. 97-98.
[6]Ibid., pp. 106-107.
[7]Ibid., pp. 118-119.
[8]Ibid., p. 119.
[9]Ibid., pp. 140-143.

Chapter Five: Choice

[1]Abraham Maslow, *The Farther Reaches of Human Nature.* (New York: Viking Press, 1971), pp. 45-50.

[2]Kurt Lewin, *Field Theory in Social Science.* (New York: Harper & Row, 1951), pp. 228-229.

[3]P. Hersey and K. H. Blanchard, *Management of Organizational Behavior.* (Englewood Cliffs, N.J.: Prentice-Hall, 1977), pp. 280-285.

Chapter Six: Support

[1]K. B. Nuckols, et al., "Psychosocial Assets, Life Crises, and the Prognosis of Pregnancy." *American Journal of Epidemiology.* Vol. 95, No. 5 (1972): pp. 431-441.

[2]L. F. Beekman and S. Syme, "Social Networks, Host Resistance, and Mortality: a Nine-Year Follow-up Study of Alameda County Residents." *American Journal of Epidemiology.* Vol. 109, No. 2 (1979): pp. 186-204.

[3]S. Gore, "The Effect of Social Support in Moderating, and Health Consequences of Unemployment." *Journal of Health and Social Behavior.* Vol. 19 (June, 1978): pp. 157-165.

[4]S. Wolf and N. Goodell, *Behavioral Science in Clinical Medicine.* (Springfield, Ill.: Charles C. Thomas, 1976), pp. 16-19, 162-173.

[5]G. W. Brown et al., "Social Class and Psychiatric Disturbance Among Women in an Urban Population." *Sociology.* Vol. 9, No. 2 (May, 1975): pp. 225-254.

[6]E. J. Langer and J. Rodin, "The Effects of Choice and Enhanced Personal Responsibility For the Aged: A Field Experiment in an Institutional Setting." *Journal of Personality and Social Psychology.* Vol. 35, No. 12 (1977): pp. 897-902.

Chapter Seven: Exercise

[1]R. S. Brown, et al., "The Prescription of Exercise For Depression." *Physicians Sports Medicine.* Vol. 6, No. 12 (1978): pp. 35-41.

[2]J. F. Aloia, et al., "Prevention of Involutional Bone Loss by Exercise." *Annals of Internal Medicine.* Vol. 89, No. 3 (Sept., 1978): pp. 356-358.

Chapter Eight: Meditation
[1]Edmund Jacobsen, *You Must Relax.* (New York: Pocket Books, 1945), p. 32.
[2]Kenneth Pelletier, *Mind As Healer, Mind As Slayer.* (New York: Dell, 1977), pp. 197-208.

Chapter Nine: Relaxation and Biofeedback
[1]Herbert Benson, *The Relaxation Response.* (New York: Avon, 1974), pp. 83-140.
[2]Kenneth Pelletier, *Mind As Healer, Mind As Slayer.* (New York: Dell, 1977), p. 224.
[3]O. Carl Simonton, Stephanie Matthews-Simonton, and James Creighton, *Getting Well Again.* (Los Angeles: J. B. Tarcher, 1978), pp. 94-163.
[4]L. John Mason, *Guide to Stress Reduction.* (Culver City, Calif.: Peace Press, 1980), p. 52.
[5]Marvin Karlins and Lewis M. Andrews, *Biofeedback: Turning on the Power of Your Mind.* (New York: Warner Books, 1972), pp. 61-62.
[6]Ibid., p. 62.
[7]Ibid., pp. 57-58.
[8]Ibid., pp. 75-76.

Chapter Ten: Purpose and Meaning
[1]M. Scott Peck, *The Road Less Traveled.* (New York: Simon and Schuster, 1978), p. 16.
[2]Carl Rogers and Barry Stevens, *Person to Person: The Problem of Being Human.* (Lafayette, Calif.: Real People Press, 1967), pp. 19-26.
[3]Ibid., p. 21.
[4]Ibid., pp. 25-26.
[5]Peck, *The Road Less Traveled,* pp. 18-68.
[6]Rollo May, *Man's Search For Himself.* (New York: W. W. Norton, 1953), p. 192.
[7]Peck, *The Road Less Traveled,* p. 260.

[6]Rollo May, *Man's Search For Himself* (New York: W. W. Norton, 1953), p. 192.
[7]Peck, *The Road Less Traveled*, p. 260.

BIBLIOGRAPHY

Alain. *Yoga for Perfect Health.* New York: Pyramid Books, 1961.

Alberti, R. E., and M. L. Emmons. *Your Perfect Right: A Guide to Assertive Behavior.* 3d ed. San Luis Obispo, Calif.: Impact, 1978.

Aloia, J. F., et al. "Prevention of Involutional Bone Loss by Exercise." *Annals of Internal Medicine.* Vol. 89, No. 3 (Sept., 1978).

Anonymous. *Each Day a New Beginning.* Center City, Minn.: Hazelden Educational Materials, 1982.

Anonymous. *The Twelve Steps: A Healing Journey.* Center City, Minn.: Hazelden Educational Materials, 1986.

Beattie, Melody. *Codependent No More.* Center City, Minn.: Hazelden Educational Materials, 1987.

Beekman, L. F., and S. Syme. "Social Networks, Host Resistance, and Mortality: A Nine-year Follow-up Study of Alameda County Residents." *American Journal of Epidemiology.* Vol. 109, No. 2 (1979).

Benson, H. *The Relaxation Response.* New York: Avon Books, 1974.

Brown, G. W., et al. "Social Class and Psychiatric Disturbances Among Women in an Urban Population." *Sociology.* Vol. 9, No. 2 (May, 1975).

Brown, R. S., et al. "The Prescription of Exercise for Depression." *Physicians Sports Medicine.* Vol. 6, No. 12 (Dec., 1978).

California Department of Mental Health. "Friends Can be Good Medicine." San Francisco: Pacificon Productions, 1981.

———. "Friends Can be Good Medicine: A Resource Guide." Edited by Lisa Hunter, San Francisco: Pacificon Productions, 1981.

———. "Can Friends Help You Stay Well?" San Francisco: Pacificon Productions, 1981.

Carter, H., and P. Glick. *Marriage and Divorce: A Social and Economic Study.* (American Public Health Association Vital and Health Statistics Monograph). Cambridge, Mass.: Harvard University Press, 1970.

Casey, K., and M. Vanceburg. *The Promise of a New Day.* Center City, Minn.: Hazelden Educational Materials, 1983.

Clinebell, H. *Mental Health Through Christian Community.* Nashville, Tenn.: Abingdon Press, 1968.

Cooper, K. *The Aerobic Program for Total Well-Being.* New York: M. Evans and Co., 1982.

Corey, G. *I Never Knew I Had a Choice.* 2d ed. Monterey, Calif.: Brooks/Cole Publishing Co., 1983.

Dass, R. *Journey of Awakening: A Meditator's Guidebook.* New York: Bantam, 1978.

Erikson, E. *Childhood and Society.* New York: W. W. Norton and Co., 1963.

Frankl, V. *Man's Search for Meaning.* New York: Washington Square Press, 1963. (Pocket Books edition, 1955).

Friedman, M., and R. Rosenman. *Type A Behavior and Your Heart.* New York: Alfred A. Knopf, 1974.

————. and C. Thoreson, et al. "Feasibility of Altering Type A Behavior Pattern After Myocardial Infarction." *Circulation.* Vol. 66, No. 1, (July, 1982).

————. and D. Ulmer. *Treating Type A Behavior and Your Heart.* New York: Alfred A. Knopf, 1984.

Fromm, E. *The Art of Loving.* New York: Harper & Row, 1956.

Glasser, W. *Positive Addiction.* New York: Harper & Row, 1976.

Gore, S. "The Effect of Social Support Moderating, and Health Consequences of Unemployment." *Journal of Health and Social Behavior.* Vol. 19, (June, 1978).

Gorski, Terence T., and Merlene Miller. *Counseling for Relapse Prevention.* Independence, Mo.: Independence Press, 1982.

Gorski, Terence T. and Merlene Miller. *Staying Sober.* Independence, Mo.: Independence Press, 1986.

Gould, R. L. *Transformations: Growth and Change in Adult Life.* New York: Simon and Schuster (Touchstone Book), 1978.

Harvey, A. *A Journey in Ladakh.* Boston: Houghton-Mifflin Co., 1983.

Heath, W. and A. Ahsani, et al. "Exercise Training Improves Lipoprotein Lipid Profiles in Patients With Coronary Artery Disease." *American Heart Journal.* Vol. 105, No. 6 (June, 1983).

Hersey, P. and K. H. Blanchard. *Management of Organizational Behavior.* Englewood, N.J.: Prentice-Hall Co., 1977.

Holmes, T. H., and R. H. Rahe. "The Social Readjustment Rating Scale." *Journal of Psychosomatic Research.* Vol. 11 (1967).

Jacobson, E. *You Must Relax.* New York: Pocket Books, 1945.

Jampolsky, G. *Teach Only Love.* New York: Bantam Books, 1983.

Johnson, C. *Windows to the Sky.* Norwalk, Conn.: C. P. Gibson Co., 1968.

Jourard, S. *The Transparent Self: Self-Disclosure and Well-being.* 2d ed. New York: Van Nostrand, 1971.

Karlins, M., and L. Andrews. *Biofeedback: Turning On the Power of Your Mind.* New York: Warner Books, 1972.

Kopp, S. *If You Meet the Buddha on the Road, Kill Him!* New York: Bantam, 1972.

Kubler-Ross, E. *On Death and Dying.* New York: Macmillan Co., 1969.

———. *Death: The Final Stage of Growth.* Englewood Cliffs, N.J.: Prentice-Hall, 1975.

Kurtz, Ernest. *Not-God: A History of Alcoholics Anonymous.* Center City, Minn.: Hazelden Educational Materials, 1979.

Kushner, H. *When Bad Things Happen to Good People.* New York: Schoken Books, 1981.

Langer, E. J., and J. Rodin. "The Effects of Choice and Enhanced Personal Responsibility for the Aged: A Field Experiment in an Institutional Setting." *Journal of Personality and Social Psychology.* Vol. 35, No. 12 (1977).

Leon, A. "Approximate Energy Expenditures and Fitness Value of Sports and Recreational and Household Activities." Laboratory of Physiological Hygiene, School of Public Health, University of Minnesota.

LeShan, L. *You Can Fight for Your Life.* New York: M. Evans and Co., 1977.

Lewin, K. *Field Theory in Social Science.* New York: Harper & Row, 1951.

Lindbergh, A. *Gift From the Sea.* New York: Pantheon, 1955.

Maslow, A. *Religions, Values and Peak Experiences.* New York: Viking Press, 1964.

———. *Toward a Psychology of Being.* 2d ed. New York: Harper & Row, 1970.

———. *Motivation and Personality.* 2d ed. New York, Harper & Row, 1970.

———. *The Farther Reaches of Human Nature.* New York: Viking Press, 1971.

Mason, L. J. *Guide to Stress Reduction.* Culver City, Calif.: Peace Press, 1980.

Mattiessen, P. *The Snow Leopard.* New York: Viking Press, 1978.

May, R. *Man's Search for Himself.* New York: W. W. Norton and Co., 1953.

———. *Love and Will.* New York: Norton, 1969, Dell, 1974.

Miller, Merlene, and Terence T. Gorski. *Family Recovery: Growing Beyond Addiction.* Independence, Mo.: Independence Press, 1982.

Miller, Merlene, Terence T. Gorski, and David K. Miller. *Learning to Live Again: A Guide for Recovery From Alcoholism.* Independence, Mo.: Independence Press, 1982.

Nockolls, K. B., et al. "Psychosocial Assets, Life Crises, and the Prognosis of Pregnancy." *American Journal of Epidemiology.* Vol. 95, No. 5 (1972).

Peck, M. S. *The Road Less Traveled.* New York: Simon and Schuster, 1978.

Pelletier, K. *Mind As Healer, Mind As Slayer.* New York: Dell, 1977.

———. *Holistic Medicine.* New York: Dell (Delta/Seymour Lawrence), 1970.

Petty, J. *Apples of Gold.* Norwalk, Conn.: C. R. Gibson Co., 1962.

Pollack, M. L., J. H. Wilmore, and S. M. Fox. *Exercise in Health and Disease.* Philadelphia: W. B. Saunders Co., 1984.

Rogers, C. *On Becoming a Person.* Boston: Houghton-Mifflin, 1961.

———, and Barry Stevens. *Person to Person: The Problem of Being Human.* Lafayette, Calif.: Real People Press, 1967.

Rosellini, Gayle, and Mark Worden. *Of Course You're Angry.* Center City, Minn.: Hazelden Educational Materials, 1985.

Schultheis, R. *Bone Games.* New York, Random House, 1984.

Selye, H. *Stress Without Distress.* New York: J. B. Lippincott Co., 1974.

Sheehy, G. *Passages.* New York: E. P. Dutton and Co., 1976.

Simonton, O. C., Stephanie Matthews-Simonton, and James Creighton. *Getting Well Again.* Los Angeles: J. C. Tarcher, Inc., 1978.

Smith, R. D., and C. Sherman. "Change of Heart: Transforming Type A's into Type B's." *American Health.* July/August, 1982.

Stearns, A. K. *Living Through Personal Crisis.* Chicago: The Thomas More Press, 1984.

Thoreson, C. E., and Meyer Friedman. "Altering the Type A Behavior Pattern in Post Infarction Patients." *Journal of Cardiopulmonary Rehabilitation.* Vol. 5, No. 6 (June, 1985).

Waters, F. *The Book of the Hopi.* New York: Viking Press (Penguin Books, Ltd.), 1963 and 1977.

Watson, L. *Gifts of Unknown Things.* New York: Simon and Schuster, 1976.

Westberg, G. E. *Good Grief.* Philadelphia: Fortress Press, 1962.

Wilson, H., and C. Kneisl. *Psychiatric Nursing.* 2d ed. Menlo Park, Calif.: Addison-Wesley, 1983.

Wolf, S., and H. Goodell. *Behavioral Science in Clinical Medicine.* New York: Charles C. Thomas, 1976.

Zohman, L. "Beyond Diet . . . Exercise Your Way to Fitness and Heart Health." Englewood Cliffs, N.J.: CPC International.

INDEX

Adaptation, SEE: Stress, adaptation; General adaptation response
Addiction,
    cross addiction, 45-46
    family response, 46-47
    SEE: Relapse
Alcoholics Anonymous, 3, 36, 44, 47, 67, 68, 112
    the Twelve Steps of A.A., 123
Anger, 15-17, 29, 30-32
    communication of, 15, 19-22
    controlling anger, 18-22
    as normal emotion, 15-16
    and recovery, 15-16, 29
    types of anger, 16-17
    SEE: Hostility; Grief; Communication
Autogenic training, 97, 98-99
Autosuggestion, SEE: Hypnosis
Behaviors,
    aggressive/passive/assertive, 18-19
    confrontation, 23
Benson, Herbert, 97
Berger, Hans, 108
Bernard, Claude, 3
Biofeedback, 91-92, Chapter 9 (97-110)
Cannon, Walter, 3
Chemical dependency, 2-3, 5, 29, 33-34, 56, 120
    SEE: Anger; Recovery; Relapse
Co-addiction, SEE: Addiction, family response
Communication, 19-23, 71-72
    characteristics, 22-23
    and confrontation skills, 23
Change, 27, 49, 54-59, 63-64
    SEE: Lewin, Kurt; Grief
Courage, 116-117

Counseling, 24-25, 33, 36-37, 40, 45, 47
Cross addiction, SEE: Addiction
Denial, 17, 29, 43, 44, 56
Depression, 15, 29-32, 36, 62
    SEE: Feelings; Grief; Guilt
Desensitization, SEE: Fear
Discipline, 115-116
Disease, 7, 16, 17, 30, 62, 107
    and change, 7, 62
Divorce, 27-28, 28-29, 36
Exercise, 36, 42, Chapter 7 (79-90)
    aerobic, 80, 87-90
    anaerobic, 80
    emotional benefits, 81-82
    establishing an exercise program, 83-90
    level of fitness, 83-86
    physchosocial benefits, 82-83
    physical assessment, 83-84
    physical benefits, 82
    types of exercise, 80-81
Fear, 36
    desensitization, 105-106
Fight or Flight Response, 3, 50, 93, 95, 98
    and physical change, 3-4
Friedman, Meyer, 17
Friendships, SEE: Relationships
General adaptation response, 5
Gorski, Terrence, 22, 41, 43, 46-47
Grief, Chapter 3 (27-37), 63
    factors affecting grief, 32-33
    grief process, 29-33
    and recovery, 33-34
    unhealthy expression of grief, 34-36
Group participation, 67-70
    and change, 56-57
    therapy, 69

Guilt, 29, 30, 32, 36
Health, 40, 42, 62
Holmes, Thomas, 8, 10
Holmes and Rahe Social Readjustment Scale, 8-9, 27-28
Homeostasis, 3, 4
Hostility, Chapter 2 (13-25), 36
    as component of Type A behavior, 17-18
    hostility quiz, 13-15
    SEE: Anger
Hypnosis,
    self-hypnosis, 97, 99-101
    visualization, 97, 101-105
    and healing, 104-105
Illness, SEE: Disease
Jacobson, Edmund, 93, 94
Johnson, Virginia, 106
Kamiya, Joe, 108-109
Lewin, Kurt, 54-55
Living in the present, 118-120
Love, 117-118
Maslow, Abraham, 49, 50, 51, 52
Hierarchy of needs (chart), 50
Masters, William, 106
May, Rollo, 112, 116-117
Meditation, 51, Chapter 8 (91-96)
    benefits, 95-96
    visualization, 97
    SEE: Hypnosis
Menninger Foundation, 109
MET, 86-87
Milieu interieur, 3
Miller, David, 22
Miller, Merlene, 22, 41, 43, 46-47
Needs,
    physical, 50
    pyschological, 50

self-actualization, 49-52, 114
Nutrition, 36, 40, 42
Pain, 6-7, 107, 109-110
    SEE: Stress, and chronic pain
Peck, M. Scott, 24, 112, 115, 121
Pelletier, Kenneth, 5
Physical fitness, SEE: Exercise
Quieting response, 98
Rahe, Richard, 8, 10
Recovery, 2-3
    and anger, 15-16
    and exercise, 81, 90
Relapse, 2-3, 29, Chapter 4 (39-47)
    and compulsive behavior, 46
    and the family, 46
    SEE: Withdrawal
Relationships, Chapter 6 (61-78)
    barriers to friendship, 72-74
    communication skills, 71-72
    personal assessment as friend, 70
    and stress, 76-78
    as support network, 74-78
    types and characteristics of, 64-67
Relaxation, Chapter 9 (97-110)
    and meditation, Chapter 8 (91-96)
    the relaxation response, 97-98
    techniques, 5
Progressive Relaxation technique, 93-94
Religion, SEE: Spirituality
Rest, 40, 42
Rogers, Carl, 112, 114-115
Rosellini, Gayle, 23
Rosenman, Ray H., 17
Schultz, Johannes, 98
Self-actualization, SEE: Needs, self-actualization

Self-awareness, 52-53, 58-59
    visualization, 53-54
Self-discipline, 115-116
Selye, Hans, 3, 5
Serenity, 119-122
Sharkey, Brian, 84
    physical activity index (table), 84-85
Spirituality, 33, 36, Chapter 10 (111-123)
    SEE: Meditation
Stress, Chapter 1 (1-11), 16, 95, 98
    adaptation to, 3-5
    and chronic pain, 5, 6, 107
    and disease, 2, 5
    and exercise, SEE: Exercise
    SEE: Stress management; Type A syndrome; Withdrawal;
Relationships, and stress
Stress management, 2-3, 31-32, 79, 91, 122
    and chemical dependency recovery, 2, 40, 47
    SEE: Exercise; Fight or Flight Response; Holmes and Rahe
Social Readjustment Scale; Meditation; Spirituality;
Twelve Steps
Stroebel, Charles, 98
Support network, Chapter 6 (61-78)
    personal network worksheet, 75-78
    SEE: Relationships
Therapy, SEE: Counseling
Transcendental meditation, 94, 97
    SEE: Meditation
Type A and Type B behaviors, 17-18, 19, 98
Twelve Steps, 3, 36, 39, 40, 42, 44-45, 112, 121, 122
    the Twelve Steps of A.A., 123
    SEE: Alcoholics Anonymous
Visualization
    SEE: Meditation; Hypnosis
Wellness, 7-8
Wellness Continuum (chart), 7-8

Withdrawal, 39-43
    coping with withdrawal, 42-43
    triggered by stress, 41
    symptoms, 40, 41-43
Wolpe, Joseph, 106
Worden, Mark, 23
Yoga, 94, 105
Zen, 94